❧ "The philosopher and father of economics Adam Smith famously wrote that 'little else' is needed for a society to prosper and progress beyond three conditions: 'peace, easy taxes, and a tolerable administration of justice.' *Peace, Love, & Liberty* is an engaging collection of essays showing why peace is the first among these indispensable conditions, and how its absence raises taxes and threatens justice. The authors argue with persuasive logic and evidence that a belligerent state cannot continue to be a free state."

Lawrence H. White
Author, *The Clash of Economic Ideas*
Department of Economics, George Mason University

❧ "*Peace, Love, & Liberty* gathers experts in economics, political science, history, philosophy, psychology, and other fields to explain the complex phenomena of peace and war. Tom Palmer as editor and author has produced a book that is truly unique and succeeds splendidly. It is rigorous and clearly written and deserves to be read by a very large audience. If the lessons of the book had been understood in the last century, the world would have been spared so much violence, blood, suffering, and misery."

Pascal Salin
Author, *Libéralisme*
Faculty of Economics, Université Paris–Dauphine

❧ "The sociologist Charles Tilly famously stated that 'War made the state and the state made war.' This neat little anthology illustrates the wisdom of those words and why any freedom-loving person should oppose all use of the destructive forces of the state for anything but self-defense."

Peter Kurrild-Klitgaard
Department of Political Science
University of Copenhagen

PEACE, LOVE, & LIBERTY

WAR IS NOT INEVITABLE

෨

This book is dedicated to the memory of John Blundell, a member of the board of directors of the Atlas Network and a pioneer of the global liberty movement. John understood the importance of freedom of trade for peace and was a steadfast advocate of free trade through his work as general director of the London-based Institute of Economic Affairs, as president of the Institute for Humane Studies at George Mason University, and as president and later board member of the Atlas Network. The editor of this book acknowledges the help, encouragement, support, and friendship of John over several decades. Peace, Love, & Liberty would not have been possible without him.

PEACE, LOVE, & LIBERTY

WAR IS NOT INEVITABLE

Edited by Tom G. Palmer

AtlasNetwork.org

StudentsForLiberty.org

JAMESON BOOKS, INC.
Ottawa, Illinois

Published by Students For Liberty & Atlas Network / Jameson Books, Inc.

Edited by Tom G. Palmer
Cover Design by Robyn Patterson

The editor gratefully acknowledges the assistance in preparing this book,
not only of the authors and copyright holders, but of the countless active
members of the Atlas Network and of Students For Liberty. Their dedication
to liberty and peace on every continent is both a great service to all those at
risk from organized violence and an inspiration to me.

For information and other requests please write:

Students For Liberty, 1101 17th St. NW, Suite 810, Washington, DC 20036

The Atlas Network, 1201 L St. NW, Washington, DC 20005

Jameson Books, Inc., 722 Columbus Street, PO Box 738, Ottawa, IL 61350
800-426-1357 for book orders.

Printed in the United States of America.

ISBN: 978-0-89803-176-8

17   16   15   14   5   4   3   2   1

CONTENTS

*Note: An index for the volume is available at
http://studentsforliberty.org/peace-love-liberty-index*

PREFACE

"People must learn to hate, and if they can learn to hate, they can be taught to love, for love comes more naturally to the human heart than its opposite."[1]   —Nelson Mandela

War teaches people to hate. Hate our enemies. Hate our neighbors. Hate those who are different. Peace allows people to love. To change enemies into friends. To replace conflict with cooperation. To replace hatred with love and friendship.

What fosters peace? The evidence is in: liberty. What undermines liberty? The evidence for that is in, too: war.

The essays in this book offer evidence and arguments for peace. The writers advance peace not merely as a moral ideal or even a desirable goal, but as an eminently practical objective. Too often peace activists have thought it sufficient merely to call for peace and to denounce war, without considering what institutions foster peace and discourage war and without investigating the economic, social, political, and psychological conditions of peace. They may oppose this or that war, without considering what causes wars and addressing those causes. Peace is not an impractical fantasy, nor is it something for which one must sacrifice prosperity or progress or freedom. In fact, peace, freedom, prosperity, and progress go hand-in-hand.

The essays in this book appeal to the mind. They are anchored in sound history, economic reality, empirical psychology, political science, and hard-headed logic, as well as art and the aesthetic imagination. If the heart is to be engaged on behalf of peace, it should be engaged through the mind.

The authors in *Peace, Love, & Liberty* draw on the disciplines of psychology, economics, political science, history, law, sociology, moral philosophy, as well as poetry, literature, and aesthetics. All play important roles in better understanding war and peace. Each essay in the book can be read profitably on its own. They may be read in any order. Some are scholarly and some, while equally serious, do not rely on footnotes. The goal has been to make important issues accessible to a wide range of interested readers while using reason and evidence to show the deep interconnection between liberty and peace. (There is more on peace and liberty than on love for a simple reason; peace and liberty are something for which one can strive in an organized fashion, whereas love is something each human heart must achieve on its own. Accordingly, the essays focus on the institutions and the ideologies of war and peace, in the hope that peace will be chosen, hatred avoided, and love made possible.)

Peace, Love, & Liberty is co-published by the Atlas Network and the Students For Liberty. Both organizations are global in scope and have affiliates and projects on every continent. They are attached to no government. They stand for universal values. They promote no agenda other than peace, equal liberty, and equal justice before law. They seek to institute and support the institutions that make peace, liberty, and justice possible, including constitutional limits on governments, freedom of speech and religion, protection of justly acquired property, legal toleration for peaceful behavior, and free trade and free markets. The essays in this book show how those ideas—the ideas of "classical liberalism" (or "libertarianism" in some countries)—cohere and reinforce each other. The essays that make up *Peace, Love, & Liberty* offer a contribution to peace studies from the perspective of libertarian (or classical liberal) scholarship and thinking, a tradition that is about the protection of voluntary human cooperation.[2]

The roots of that tradition run deep in human history. They are discernible in the writings of the Chinese sage Lao Tse, of the great religious leaders, and of a great lawyer, philosopher, and politician who upheld eloquence and reason over brutality and force, Marcus Tullius Cicero. As he wrote in his famous book *On Duties*,

> All men should have this one object, that the benefit of each individual and the benefit of all together should be the same. If anyone arrogates it to himself, all human intercourse will be dissolved. Furthermore, if nature prescribes that one man should want to consider the interests of another, whoever he

may be, for the very reason that he is a man, it is necessary, according to the same nature, that what is beneficial to all is something common. If that is so, then we are all constrained by one and the same law of nature; and if that also is true, then we are certainly forbidden by the law of nature from acting violently against another person.[3]

This book is about avoiding violence. It is about the peaceful alternative to force. It is about voluntary cooperation. It is dedicated to activists for peace and liberty everywhere. I hope that the youth of today may grow old in peace and freedom and that they may leave the world more peaceful, more just, and with far more liberty than they found it. For those who share that goal, the information in this book will be helpful.

Tom G. Palmer
Nairobi, Kenya

**Note: An index for the volume is available at
http://studentsforliberty.org/peace-love-liberty-index**

1

Peace Is a Choice

By Tom G. Palmer

What is the nature of war? Is it an irreducible feature of human life? Is it justified and, if it is, under what conditions? What is the impact of war on morality and on liberty?

"A universal and perpetual peace, it is to be feared, is in the catalogue of events, which will never exist but in the imaginations of visionary philosophers, or in the breasts of benevolent enthusiasts. It is still however true, that war contains so much folly, as well as wickedness, that much is to be hoped from the progress of reason; and if any thing is to be hoped, every thing ought to be tried." —James Madison[4]

Wars don't just happen. They're not like tornados or meteors, and not merely because they can be far more destructive. The more important difference is that tornados and meteors don't result from human deliberation and choice. Wars do. There are ideologies that promote war. There are policies that make wars more likely. And those ideologies and policies can be examined, compared, and discussed rationally. One may think that "everyone favors peace," but one would be wrong. Many ideologies have conflict and violence at their very core. And even if their advocates publicly say they oppose war and prefer peace, the policies they advocate make far more likely the eruption of such conflicts into war. As James Madison, one of the great figures of the American Enlightenment and primary author of the Constitution of the United States, noted, war "contains so much folly, as well as wickedness," that we must try what we can to reduce it.

What can one say about war that hasn't already been said? I just entered the term "war" in the Google search engine and in .49 seconds I received this response: "About 536,000,000 results." And that's just in English. In .23 seconds I got "About 36,700,000 results" in French (guerre); in .30 seconds I got "About 14,700,000 results" in German (Krieg); and in Chinese in .38 seconds I got "About 55,900,000 results" in simplified characters (战争) and in .34 seconds "About 6,360,000 results" in traditional characters (戰爭). What more could possibly be added to that?

Something very important *can* be added to all of that. *More reason* should be introduced into the discussion. As Madison suggests, "Much is to be hoped from the progress of reason."

War Is Organized Human Violence

A common dictionary definition of war is "a state of armed conflict between different nations or states or different groups within a nation or state." Examples of its use would be: "Austria waged war on Italy" and "There was a war between Austria and Italy." The word may also be used analogously or metaphorically; thus, "He was at war with his neighbors" and "The government launched a war on drugs." The primary use of war, however, and the primary use in this book, refers to armed conflict between states. (That said, the "war on drugs" also involves a great deal of armed conflict, but normally directed by states against drug suppliers and consumers, and among rival drug distributors, rather than among states.)

"Armed conflict" makes it clear that deadly force is used. In wars, people die. But really, they don't just die. They are killed by other people. War and the use of military force both involve killing people. Military men and women know that truth. Politicians often want to avoid it. Madeleine Albright, then US Ambassador to the United Nations and later US Secretary of State, famously asked then US chairman of the Joint Chiefs of Staff, General Colin L. Powell, "What's the point of having this superb military you're always talking about if we can't use it?"

Powell wrote in his memoirs, "I thought I would have an

aneurysm." And well he might. Albright had a common understanding of military force as just another tool of state to be deployed to realize her agenda. Powell explained that "American GIs were not toy soldiers to be moved around on some sort of global game board" and that "we should not commit military forces until we had a clear political objective." As a military man General Powell understood that when you "use" military forces, real human beings, not toy soldiers or chess pieces, are going to be killed.[5]

I recall sitting down years ago with Rear Admiral Gene LaRoque (USN, Ret.) and talking about the use of military force. He explained in very direct language (I draw from memory): "The purpose of the armed forces is to kill the enemy and to destroy his ability to harm us. We don't build bridges well, unless your goal is to drive tanks across them. We don't know how to teach 8-year-olds to read and write. We don't know how to educate people about law or democracy. We kill the enemy and we destroy his ability to harm us. And when you really have to kill people and destroy things, call on us, but otherwise, don't." Going to war means killing other human beings. The ones who tend not to talk about it casually are the ones who had to see—or do—it up close.

People who have seen wars tend to think about them very differently than political science professors such as Madeleine Albright, who as a US government official publicly and very eagerly defended the bombing of Iraq, which led to the deaths of many innocent people. At a public forum in the United States about war with Iraq, she was challenged by a citizen. "We will not send messages to Saddam Hussein with the blood of the Iraqi people," he said. "If you want to deal with Saddam, deal with Saddam, not the Iraqi people." Her response was revealing:

What we are doing is so that you all can sleep at night. I am very proud of what we are doing. We are the greatest nation in the world, [pause for applause] and what we are doing, is being the indispensable nation, willing to make the world safe for our children and grandchildren, and for nations who follow the rules.[6]

Albright and her colleagues defended bombing Iraqis and enforcing an embargo that led to substantial loss of life to fill the role of "the indispensable nation" and "to make the world safe for our children and grandchildren." She and her colleagues didn't get their chance to invade Iraq, which was carried out by their successor, George W. Bush and his administration, but they did throw their support to the destructive and expensive folly carried out by the Bush administration. Were those decisions justified? In fact, they were not. They did not discharge the burden required to make their case. There was no solid evidence that the Iraqi state was developing "weapons of mass destruction" that could be deployed "within forty-five minutes" of the order being given, nor was there any evidence that the regime had been involved in the terrorist attacks on American citizens of September 11, 2001, despite claims made by government officials to the public that implied such involvement.

And what was the cost? Deriving precise numbers in the Iraqi case is difficult and a matter of much dispute, but in addition to the tens of thousands of Iraqi combatants killed in the invasion, there were the thousands of US, British, and allied soldiers killed, and many tens of thousands wounded. At least (on a conservative estimate) 118,789 civilians were killed violently from 2003 to 2011, most of them victims of the horrifyingly brutal civil war and power struggle within the country set off by the invasion and occupation.[7]

And what of the loss of wealth? The US government alone borrowed some $2 trillion to finance the wars in Iraq and Afghanistan (the two are not easy to disentangle due to their overlapping durations) and the total cost of those two adventures, reckoned in present value terms, is very conservatively estimated at $4 trillion, but almost certainly much more.[8] Britain and other countries also expended substantial sums of material wealth and the infrastructure of Iraq was seriously damaged in the conflict. Was all that expenditure of lives and treasure to produce so much death and destruction justified?

When, If Ever, Is War Justified?

Few people believe that going to war—killing people—is justified in order to "be the indispensable nation," as Albright maintained.

8

(Some, however, would defend that position.) But let's take the harder case. If a war is undertaken "to make the world safe for our children and grandchildren," is it justified then? Facts would surely be important to answering this question: "What is the likelihood that killing people today will make others safer in the future?" Perhaps such killing *would* make us safer in the future, but there would still have to be a very substantial burden of proof on the advocate of going to war. The advocates of war between the US government and the government of Iraq did not begin to meet that burden of proof.

There is a long tradition of judging the justice of wars, both their initiation and their conduct. The justification of going to war is known in Latin as *jus ad bellum* and is distinguished from the justice of the conduct of war, called *jus in bello*. Those two topics are frequently considered as separate matters. Is the war justified and is the behavior undertaken to prosecute the war justified? Many great lawyers and philosophers have argued and debated about what might justify going to war and, once war is begun, whether there are moral or legal restraints on the use of force and, if so, what they are.

May one initiate a war to defend the honor of a ruler or a nation, or to "be the indispensable nation," or to seize valuable land or resources, or to defend one's interests or the lives of a nation's people? And, once war is undertaken, may one kill only armed combatants in the field, or may one execute captured prisoners, or may one kill the families of enemy soldiers, including their children (who may be future soldiers)? Over time, more and more limits were placed on the occasions for war, and various principles, conventions, and treaties were established to regulate the conduct of war.

Taken together, the topics are known as the "law of war" and "just war theory."[9] Although *jus in bello*, the lawfulness of the conduct of war, is considered applicable regardless of whether a war is considered justified, the standard approach has been that if a war is justified, that is, undertaken for a just cause, then the means necessary to its successful conduct are themselves justified, even if undesirable in themselves or regrettable.

But for those who care about justice, about behaving rightly, that traditional approach cannot adequately address whether going to war (*jus ad bellum*) is justified. As Robert Holmes has forcefully argued in his book *On War and Morality*, "It is not the end that justifies the means but the permissibility of the means (including the killing and destroying that are part of the nature of warfare) that, along with satisfaction of the other requirements of *jus ad bellum*, justifies the end."[10] Not only "evil doers" are killed in wars. Completely innocent people become "collateral damage," as well. If killing people and destroying what they need to survive are not justified, then the process—the war—is not justified either. Thus, "To justify going to war requires justifying the selection of means from the outset. There are not two separate acts here, the embarking upon war and the implementing of chosen means. . . . One can never justify the resort to war without justifying the means by which one proposes to fight the war."[11]

When considering war, it is morally irresponsible to look only at the ostensible goal of the war, whether the retaking of historical territory or the vindication of honor or the establishment of credibility or the response to aggression or any other cause, without considering just what the war will entail. As Holmes affirms, "War by its nature is organized violence, the deliberate, systematic causing of death and destruction. This is true whether the means employed are nuclear bombs or bows and arrows."[12]

I came face to face with the common avoidance of this very issue some ten years ago when I was working in war-torn Iraq and flew to Canada for a conference. A conference participant informed me of how sorry she was that Canada had not taken part in the "Coalition of the Willing" that invaded Iraq and toppled the tyrannical and murderous government of Saddam Hussein and his Baathist Party. I told her she should be glad that her government had deliberated and had chosen *not* to be a part of the invasion and occupation.

Later in the discussion, I mentioned the "talk on the street" in Baghdad that the new Iraqi police had been instructed to shoot people who were captured laying Improvised Explosive Devices (IEDs) and that a high government official had demonstrated the government's resolve by shooting a prisoner himself. IEDs were at the time killing large numbers of combatants and noncombatants alike. (I didn't—and don't—know whether the story was true. I merely reported what a number of Iraqis with whom I had spoken had told me.) The same person who had eagerly supported Canada joining the war effort was shocked, appalled, and horrified and demanded that "something be done." I told her that she should have considered the likelihood of such outcomes before endorsing going to war. It's the kind of thing that "happens" during war. It shows a lack of understanding to endorse a war and then express shock when it entails violent, bloody, and even lawless behavior.

War not only leads to unintended casualties that are somehow not reckoned in the decision whether to go to war, but it changes human character. Not only do some combatants lose their moral compass, but noncombatants do, as well. Joe Klein is a respected journalist for *Time* magazine who is a supporter of President Obama. In defense of the Obama administration's use of drone strikes in a television discussion program, he hotly stated,

> If it is misused, and there is a really major possibility of abuse if you have the wrong people running the government. But: the bottom line in the end is—whose 4-year-old gets killed? What we're doing is limiting the possibility that 4-year-olds here will get killed by indiscriminate acts of terror.[13]

Setting aside the disturbingly obvious and smug partisanship ("There is a really major possibility of abuse if you have the wrong people running the government"), it is hard to imagine such a cold-hearted defense of killing 4-year-old children, but Mr. Klein was unapologetic. People lose their moral compasses when defending wars waged by "the right people."

For those and additional reasons there should be—always and everywhere—a presumption against war. The burden of proof is on the one who would initiate or engage in a war. Discharging that burden requires extremely strong reasons. Some would argue that there can never be sufficient reasons. Others argue that defensive war, or even a preemptive war against a real threat, may be justi-fied with evidence. In any case, the initiation of hostilities requires overwhelming proof and, moreover, war may be used only to defend, never to take or acquire or merely to defend "honor" or "credibility." If one is *not sure*, then the logic of the burden of proof requires that one be *against* going to war. There is no middle ground, no neutrality, no "maybe." If the case is not for war, then the case is against it. The choice is binary: for or against.

War Is the Health of the State

> *"War is the health of the state. It automatically sets in motion throughout society those irresistible forces for uniformity, for passionate cooperation with the Government in coercing into obedience the minority groups and individuals which lack the larger herd sense."* —Randolph Bourne[14]

War challenges lawfulness at every turn. It undermines the rule of law. It concentrates power in the executive branch of government. It provides a ready-to-hand justification for every abuse of power. The recent evidence of enormous spying and surveillance apparatuses of very dubious legality are a case in point. Such surveillance would have been considered the fantasy of a paranoid kook only a few years ago; and it is all justified in the name of "the war on terror."

War increases the power of government and its ability to exercise its coercive powers. With every war, new powers are gained and it takes much time and much effort to roll those powers back, if they are rolled back at all. Like other crises, it sets into motion a "ratchet effect" that increases state powers well above what preceded and, although those powers may recede after the war is concluded, they rarely fall to the level that preceded the war. As economic historian Robert Higgs explained, governments grow in response to "crises," notably wars or depressions: "Government expands the scope of its effective authority over economic decision-making with the onset of a crisis" and "the retrenchment that follows the crisis is incomplete, leaving government permanently bigger than it would have been had the crisis never occurred."[15] War paves the way for forced labor (in the form of conscription), for taxation, for confiscation and requisitioning of goods, for rationing, for socialism. New agencies, new powers, new taxes, all can be justified by alleging their need to "win the war," "defeat the enemy," and "secure the nation." War breeds collectivism and statism.

And with war come taxes and debt. As Thomas Paine dryly explained,

> War is the common harvest of all those who participate in the division and expenditure of public money, in all countries. It is the art of conquering at home: the object of it is an increase of revenue; and as revenue cannot be increased without taxes, a pretence must be made for expenditures. In reviewing the history of the English government, its wars and taxes, an observer, not blinded by prejudice, nor warped by interest, would declare that taxes were not raised to carry on wars, but that wars were raised to carry on taxes.[16]

There is nothing like a war to justify increasing the burden of taxation on the people. The history of government has demonstrated, as Margaret Levi found, that "the most acceptable justification for taxation was war."[17]

During wartime, criticism is characterized as treasonous, defeatist, and unpatriotic. Civil liberties are abandoned, censorship imposed, newspapers shut down, and spying on citizens authorized. Fellow citizens are designated enemies, demonized, harassed, arrested, interned, expelled, or killed.

Finally, war undermines accountable government. It allows rulers to pursue their own agendas under cover of pursuing the agenda of the country. It provides the means whereby political elites cement their power, divert attention away from domestic failings, and unify public opinion behind the existing rulers. William Shakespeare dramatically expressed the political impact of war in his play "Henry IV, Part II," when the old king summons his son and explains the benefits of foreign expeditions to cementing his power:

> And all my friends, which thou must make thy friends,
> Have but their stings and teeth newly ta'en out;
> By whose fell working I was first advanc'd,
> And by whose power I well might lodge a fear

To be again displac'd; which to avoid,
I cut them off; and had a purpose now
To lead out many to the Holy Land,
Lest rest and lying still might make them look
Too near unto my state. Therefore, my Harry,
Be it thy course to busy giddy minds
With foreign quarrels, that action, hence borne out
May waste the memory of the former days.[18]

To "busy giddy minds with foreign quarrels" is a regular feature of statecraft. It is not limited to the West or the East, the North or the South, democracies or dictatorships. It is a tool of power. And it often works.

Who Is Accountable?

Organized human violence has enormous costs to life, to freedom, to prosperity. A rational burden of justification is rarely met. And rarely is there any justice after war, either. The losers may be punished, but the winners almost never face justice for what they visited on their victims. That has been the case for a very long time. One of the greatest champions of constitutional government, the Roman philosopher and senator Cato the Younger, publicly rebuked one of the most famous killers of all time, Julius Caesar, for one of Caesar's atrocious war crimes in a memorable scene in the Roman Senate, as described by the historian Plutarch.

Caesar was at this time engaged with many warlike nations, and was subduing them at great hazards. Among the rest, it was believed he had set upon the Germans, in a time of truce, and had thus slain three hundred thousand of them. Upon which, some of his friends moved the senate for a public thanksgiving; but Cato declared, they ought to deliver Caesar into the hands of those who had been thus unjustly treated, and so expiate the offence and not bring a curse upon the city; "Yet we have reason," said he, "to thank the gods, for that they spared the commonwealth, and did not take vengeance upon the army, for the madness and folly of the general."[19]

Needless to say, Caesar was neither arrested nor turned over to the few survivors of his massacre. They were afforded no opportunity to punish him for the slaughter of their families. Indeed, he went on to boast proudly of his exploits in his book on the *Gallic Wars*. He wrote (using the third person to describe himself) about his organization of a surprise attack on a Germanic encampment; after detaining the leaders of the German tribe who had come to talk peace, Caesar launched a surprise attack on their people, and while his troops were massacring the unprepared men,

> the rest of the people, [consisting] of boys and women (for they had left their country and crossed the Rhine with all their families), began to fly in all directions; in pursuit of whom Caesar sent the cavalry. The Germans when, upon hearing a noise behind them, [they looked and] saw that their families were being slain, throwing away their arms and abandoning their standards, fled out of the camp, and when they had arrived at the confluence of the Meuse and the Rhine, the survivors despairing of farther escape, as a great number of their countrymen had been killed, threw themselves into the river and there perished, overcome by fear, fatigue, and the violence of the stream. Our soldiers, after the alarm of so great a war, for the number of the enemy amounted to 430,000, returned to their camp, all safe to a man, very few being even wounded.[20]

How many today remember that Julius Caesar presided over the cold-blooded butchering of hundreds of thousands of people in a single day? Only the Stoic philosopher and senator Cato rebuked him for his crime and for that Cato later paid with his life. There were prosecutions for crimes by the losing sides in World War II, but unsurprisingly rather little attention was paid to criminal misbehavior by politicians or soldiers of the victorious powers, most notably the Soviet Union, but also the Chinese governments (Kuomingtang and Communist), the United States, and the United Kingdom, the latter of which carried out some courts-martial but rarely prosecuted killings of prisoners.[21]

War is organized human violence. War is destructive, not constructive; the bringer of death, not life; the friend of unaccountable power and the enemy of liberty.

Thousands of years ago, an unknown poet wrote of a contest between two of the foundational poets of Western Civilization, Homer and Hesiod. Homer was the author of the quintessential war poem, the *Iliad*, which begins "Rage—Goddess, sing the rage of Peleus's son Achilles," and Hesiod the author of the *Works and Days*, which tells how to lead a productive and virtuous life. The poem about the poets is a work of genius; each poet is called on to recite his poetry, drawing on his famous work, one starting with a line from his poem and the other finishing it with a line from his. Hesiod's are very day-to-day, whereas Homer's are glorious. After the glory of Homer's warlike stanzas,

> all the Hellenes called for Homer to be crowned. But King Paneides bade each of them recite the finest passage from his own poems. Hesiod, therefore, began as follows [*with a passage from his poem on harvesting and ploughing*]
> "When the Pleiads, the daughters of Atlas, begin to rise, begin the harvest, and begin ploughing ere they set . . ."
> Then Homer
> [*with a passage on the glory of battle, of ranks of men standing*] "shield with shield, and helm with helm, and each man with his fellow, and the peaks of their head-pieces with crests of horsehair touched as they bent their heads . . ."

After the comparison of the two passages,

> the Hellenes applauded Homer admiringly, so far did the verses exceed the ordinary level; and demanded that he should be adjudged the winner. But the king gave the crown to Hesiod, declaring that it was right that he who called upon men to follow peace and husbandry should have the prize rather than one who dwelt on war and slaughter.[22]

It is time to celebrate the virtues of peace, of cooperation and industry, of trade and commerce, of science and knowledge, of love and beauty, of liberty and justice, and to leave behind the vices of war, of conflict and destruction, of looting and confiscating, of censoring and stifling, of hatred and horror, of coercion and lawlessness. In the modern world, the world of peace and rising prosperity, the prize should to go to those who call upon human beings to follow peace, rather than war and slaughter.

Liberty and Peace

Liberty and peace. That is what libertarians offer. Liberty and peace are a matter of choice. They have lifted up, and are lifting up, billions of people from poverty and wretchedness. The choice for liberty and peace is the right choice for mature men and women. There is courage; there is excitement; there is daring; there is greatness; and there is even a kind of glory for those who create and trade in peace, and that courage, that excitement, that daring, that greatness, and that glory are of far greater worth than the cruelly distorted mirror images of them presented by war. Entrepreneurship, prosperity, civil society, friendship, achievement, productivity, art, knowledge, beauty, love, family, satisfaction, contentment, happiness—those can be achieved in peace or destroyed in war.

To those who complain of the "boredom" of peace, to those who yearn for antagonism, conflict, and violence, the great classical liberal writer Benjamin Constant responded many years ago,

> Are we here only to build, with our dying bodies, your road to fame? You have a genius for fighting: what good is it to us? You are bored by the inactivity of peace. Why should your boredom concern us?[23]

After so much war and slaughter in human history, it is time, finally, for the prize to go to those who follow peace and husbandry, rather than those who dwell on war and slaughter.

2

THE DECLINE OF WAR AND CONCEPTIONS OF HUMAN NATURE

By Steven Pinker

It may be hard to believe, but the incidence of war is declining. What is the evidence and what are the reasons for that remarkable fact? Steven Pinker is a Johnstone Family Professor in the Department of Psychology at Harvard University. He conducts research on language and cognition, writes for publications such as the *New York Times*, *Time*, and *The New Republic*, and is the author of eight books, including *The Language Instinct*, *How the Mind Works*, *Words and Rules*, *The Blank Slate*, *The Stuff of Thought*, and most recently, *The Better Angels of Our Nature: Why Violence Has Declined.*

War appears to be in decline. In the two-thirds of a century since the end of World War II, the great powers, and developed states in general, have rarely faced each other on the battlefield, a historically unprecedented state of affairs (Holsti 1986; Jervis 1988; Luard 1988; Gaddis 1989; Mueller 1989, 2004, 2009; Ray 1989; Howard 1991; Keegan 1993; Payne 2004; Gat 2006; Gleditsch 2008; see Pinker 2011, chapter 5, for a review). Contrary to expert predictions, the United States and the Soviet Union did not launch World War III, nor have any of the great powers fought each other since the end of the Korean War in 1953. After a 600-year stretch in which

Western European countries started two new wars a year, they have not started one since 1945. Nor have the 40 or so richest nations anywhere in the world engaged each other in armed conflict. In another pleasant surprise, since the end of the Cold War in 1989, wars of all kinds have declined throughout the world (Human Security Centre 2005; Lacina, Gleditsch, and Russett 2006; Human Security Report Project 2007; Gleditsch 2008; Goldstein 2011; Human Security Report Project 2011; see Pinker 2011, chapter 6, for a review). Wars between states have become extremely rare, and civil wars, after increasing in number from the 1960s through 1990s, have declined in number. The worldwide rate of death from interstate and civil war combined has juddered downward as well, from almost 300 per 100,000 world population during World War II, to almost 30 during the Korean War, to the low teens during the era of the Vietnam War, to single digits in the 1970s and 1980s, to less than 1 in the twenty-first century.

How seriously should we take the evidence for a decline in war? Is it a statistical fluke, a gambler's lucky streak which is sure to run out? Is it an artifact of the way that wars and their human costs are counted? Is it a temporary lull in an inexorable cycle—the calm before the storm, the San Andreas Fault before the Big One, an overgrown forest awaiting the first careless toss of a lit cigarette? No one can answer those questions with certainty. In this article, I will address them via the nature of human nature.

Many observers are skeptical that war could possibly be in decline because, they say, human nature has not changed, and so we continue to harbor the innate inclinations to violence that caused the incessant warring in our history. The evidence for innate aggressive tendencies is plentiful enough: we see it in the ubiquity of aggression among primates and in the universality of violence in human societies, including homicide, rape, domestic violence, rioting, raiding, and feuding. Moreover, there is good reason to believe that certain genes, hormones, brain circuits, and selective pressures militated toward violence as our species evolved (see Pinker 2011, chapters 2, 8, and 9, for reviews). In just the two generations that have grown to adulthood since 1945, those pressures could not have gone into reverse and undone the results of several million years of hominid evolution. Since our biological impulses toward war have not gone away, according to this argument, any interlude of peace is bound to be temporary. Those who believe that the decline of war is anything but an artifact or a lucky streak are often accused of being romantics, idealists, utopians. Indeed, a few Rousseauans have pretty much accepted this argument and have denied that human nature has impulses toward violence in the first place—we are, they say, naked bonobos (the so-called hippie chimps), suffused with oxytocin and equipped with empathy neurons that naturally incline us toward peace.

I do not believe we are hippie chimps, but I do believe that the decline in war is real. As someone who is on record as being a Hobbesian realist, I am particularly suited to argue that a decline in war is compatible with a nonromantic view of human nature. In *The Blank Slate* (Pinker 2002), I argued that our brains have been shaped by natural selection to include, among other traits, greed, fear, revenge, rage, machismo, tribalism, and self-deception, which alone and in combination can incite our species to violence. Yet, I will argue that this jaded view of human nature is perfectly compatible with interpreting the decline of war as a real and possibly enduring development in human history.

Four Reasons Why the Decline of War Is Compatible with a Realistic Conception of Human Nature

1. Stranger Things Have Happened

A decline in the rate—and in some cases the existence—of a particular category of violence is by no means unusual in human history. My book *The Better Angels of Our Nature* (Pinker 2011), and James Payne's *A History of Force* (Payne 2004), document dozens of them. Here are some examples:

- Anarchic tribal societies had rates of death in warfare that were probably five times those in early settled states.
- Human sacrifice was a regular practice in every early civilization and now has vanished.
- Between the Middle Ages and the twentieth century, rates of

homicide in Europe fell at least 35-fold.

- In a Humanitarian Revolution centered in the second half of the eighteenth century, every major Western country abolished the use of torture as a form of criminal punishment.
- European countries used to have hundreds of capital crimes on the books, including trivial offenses such as stealing a cabbage and criticizing the royal garden. Beginning in the eighteenth century, capital punishment came to be reserved for treason and the most severe violent crimes, and in the twentieth century, it was abolished by every Western democracy except the United States. Even in the United States, 17 of the 50 states have abolished capital punishment, and in the remaining ones, the per capita rate of executions is a tiny fraction of what it was in colonial times.
- Chattel slavery was once legal everywhere on earth. But the eighteenth century launched a wave of abolitions that swept over the world, culminating in 1980 when slavery was abolished in Mauritania.
- Also abolished in the humanitarian revolution were witch hunts, religious persecution, dueling, blood sports, and debtors' prisons.
- Lynchings of African Americans used to take place at a rate of 150 a year. During the first half of the twentieth century, the rate fell to zero.
- Corporal punishment of children, both institutionalized paddling and whipping in schools, and spanking and smacking in households, has been in sharp decline in most Western countries and has been made illegal in several Western European countries.
- Rates of homicide, rape, domestic violence, child abuse, and hate crimes have declined dramatically (in some cases by as much as 80 percent) since the 1970s.

Given these documented declines in violence, it is pointless to argue whether human nature allows rates of violence to change. Clearly, it does; the only question is how.

2. Human Nature Has Multiple Components

People tend to reduce human nature to a single essence and then debate what that essence consists of. Are we nasty or noble, Hobbesian or Rousseauan, ape or angel? In this way of thinking, if we regularly engage in violence, we must be a violent species; if we are capable of peace we must be pacifistic.

But the brain is a mind-bogglingly complex organ with many anatomically and chemically distinguishable circuits. Most psychologists believe that human nature is not just one thing, but comprises multiple intelligences, modules, faculties, organs, drives, or other subsystems. Some of these subsystems may impel us toward violence, but others inhibit us from violence.

Human violence springs from at least four kinds of motives, each involving different neurobiological systems:

Exploitation: Violence used as the means to an end; that is, damaging a human who happens to be an obstacle on the path to something the actor wants. Examples include plunder, rape, conquest, the displacement or genocide of native peoples, and the murder or imprisonment of political or economic rivals.

Dominance: The urge among individuals to ascend the pecking order and become the alpha male, and the corresponding urge among groups for tribal, ethnic, racial, national, or religious supremacy.

Revenge: The conviction that someone who has committed a moral infraction deserves to be punished.

Ideology: Shared belief systems, spread virally or by indoctrination or force, which hold out the prospect of a utopia. Examples include nationalism, Fascism, Nazism, communism, and militant religions. Since a utopia is a world that will be infinitely good forever, one is permitted to perpetrate unlimited amounts of force against those who stand in its way, as in the saying, "You can't make an omelet without breaking a few eggs."

Pushing against these nasty impulses are some of our kinder, gentler faculties:

Self-control: Circuitry in the frontal lobes of the brain that can anticipate the long-term consequence of actions and inhibit them accordingly.

Empathy: The ability to feel someone else's pain.

The moral sense: A system of norms and taboos centered on intuitions of fairness to individuals, loyalty to a community, deference to legitimate authority, and the safeguarding of purity and sanctity. The moral sense can motivate the imposition of standards of fairness and can render certain courses of harmful action unthinkable. (Unfortunately, it can also be a cause of violence, because it can rationalize militant ideologies based on tribalism, puritanism, and authoritarianism.)

Reason: Cognitive processes that allow us to engage in objective, detached analysis.

Whether people actually commit acts of violence, then, depends on the interplay among these faculties; the mere existence of human nature does not doom our species to a constant rate of violence.

The decision to wage war, in particular, may be triggered by any combination of the violence-inducing motives. If the decision is not overturned by any of the motives that inhibit violence, the decision-maker must then mobilize an aggressive coalition by whipping up the aggressive motives in his compatriots, while disabling the peaceable motives. The actual outbreak of war thus depends on many psychological processes lining up in the right way and escaping the restraining influence of other psychological processes, which are distributed in social networks connecting many other individuals. There is no reason to expect that the relative strengths of these competing influences should remain constant over the course of human history.

3. Facultative Components of Human Nature

Many components of human nature are facultative (environmentally sensitive), not hydraulic (homeostatic). The intuition that a respite from war could not possibly be real often rests on a mental model in which the drive toward violence is conceived of as a hydraulic force. At best, it can be diverted or channeled, but it cannot be bottled up indefinitely. The hydraulic model of human motivation is deeply embedded in the way we think about violence. It was given a scientific imprimatur by psychoanalysis, ethology, and behaviorism (in the guise of drive reduction), and it fits with the cybernetic notion of homeostasis, in which a feedback loop maintains a system

23

in a steady state by counteracting any imbalance. It also fits with our subjective experience: no one can go indefinitely without food, water, or sleep, and it is a challenge to do without sex or to hold in a mounting urge to yawn, sneeze, scratch an itch, or expel various substances from the body.

But, it is a big mistake to think that all human responses are homeostatic. Many are opportunistic, reactive, or facultative: they are elicited by combinations of environmental triggers and cognitive and emotional states. Consider evolutionarily prepared fears such as those of heights, snakes, confinement, deep water, or spiders. Even if one were born with an innate phobia of snakes, as long as one never encountered a snake one could live one's entire life without experiencing that fear. Other examples include the tendency to shiver, fall head over heels in love, or experience sexual jealousy.

The motives that lead to violence, too, need not be homeostatic. There is no reason to believe that the urge to hurt someone gradually builds up and periodically needs to be discharged. Violence carries significant risks of injury or death when the target defends himself, when he or his relatives wreak revenge, or when he is tempted into attacking preemptively. The theory of natural selection predicts that adaptations evolve when their expected costs exceed their expected benefits. We should not expect a hydraulic urge to violence to evolve, but rather one that is sensitive to circumstances. These may include predation and exploitation, when an opportunity to exploit a victim at low risk presents itself; dominance, when one's masculinity is suddenly impugned in front of an important audience; vengeance, to punish (and thus ultimately deter) insults or injuries; rampage, when a longstanding menace is suddenly exposed in a window of vulnerability. If the circumstances never materialize—say, if one lives an orderly, bourgeois life, free from grave threats or insults—any tendency to react with violence could lie as dormant as a fear of poisonous snakes. The same sensitivity to environmental contingencies could, if circumstances line up, prevent political leaders from experiencing any urge to mobilize their countries for war.

4. Human Cognition Is an Open-ended Generative System

Among the various psychological faculties that can inhibit us from violence, one is special: the cognitive apparatus which makes it possible for humans to reason. Reason is a combinatorial system that can generate an explosive number of distinct thoughts. Just as the tens of thousands of words in our vocabularies can be assembled by the rules of syntax into trillions of sentences, the even greater number of concepts in our mental repertoire can be assembled by cognitive processes into an unfathomably vast number of coherent thoughts (Pinker 1994, 1997, 1999). Within this space of humanly possible ideas lie the beliefs, myths, stories, religions, ideologies, superstitions, and intuitive and formal theories that emerge from our ruminations and that propagate, via language, through our social networks, there to be further tweaked, revamped, and combined. Given the right social infrastructure—literacy, open debate, the mobility of people and ideas, a shared commitment to logical coherence and empirical testability—good science, deep mathematical truths, and useful inventions can occasionally emerge from the chatter.

Just as our species has applied its cognitive powers to ward off the scourges of pestilence and famine, so it can apply them to manage the scourge of war. After all, although the spoils of war are always tempting, sooner or later people are bound to realize that victors and losers tend to change places in the long run, and so, everyone would be better off if somehow everyone could simultaneously agree to lay down their arms. The challenge is how to get the other guy to lay down his arms at the same time that you do, because unilateral pacifism leaves a society vulnerable to invasion by its still warlike neighbors.

It requires no stretch of the imagination to suppose that human ingenuity and experience have gradually been brought to bear on this problem, just as they have chipped away at hunger and disease. Here are a few of the products of human cognition that have disincentivized leaders and populations from plunging into war:

- Government, which reduces the temptation to launch an exploitative attack, because the legal punishment cancels out the anticipated gain. This in turn reduces the temptation of a potential target to launch preemptive strikes against potential aggressors, to maintain a belligerent posture to deter them, or to wreak revenge on them after the fact.

- Limits on government, including the apparatus of democracy, so that governments do not perpetrate more violence on their citizens than they prevent.
- An infrastructure of commerce, which makes it cheaper to buy things than to plunder them and which makes other people more valuable alive than dead.
- An international community, which can propagate norms of nonviolent cooperation that are large-scale analogs of those that allow individual people to get along in their communities and workplaces.
- Intergovernmental organizations, which can encourage commerce, resolve disputes, keep belligerents apart, police infractions, and penalize aggression.
- Measured responses to aggression, including economic sanctions, quarantines, symbolic declarations, tactics of nonviolent resistance, and proportional counterstrikes as opposed to all-out retaliation.
- Reconciliation measures such as ceremonies, monuments, truth commissions, and formal apologies, which consolidate compromises among former enemies by mitigating their urge to settle every score.
- Humanistic counter-ideologies such as human rights, universal brotherhood, expanding empathy, and the demonization of war, which can compete in the intellectual marketplace with nationalism, militarism, revanchism, and utopian ideologies.

These and other cognitive gadgets seem to have whittled down the probability that the constant frictions which characterize interactions among people will ignite into an actual war (Russett and Oneal 2001; Long and Brecke 2003; Mueller 2004, 2010; Gleditsch 2008; Goldstein 2011; Human Security Report Project 2011). Many of these products of human ingenuity are invoked in the theories of the Liberal or Kantian peace, and the allusion to that Enlightenment thinker is appropriate. Like other political theorists from the Age of Reason and the Enlightenment such as Locke, Hume, and Spinoza, Kant theorized both about the conditions favoring nonviolence and the combinatorial mechanisms of human cognition. The combination of psychological and political interests is, I suggest, no coincidence.

Conclusion

Only time will tell whether the decline of war is an enduring change in the human condition, rather than a transient lull or a statistical fluke. But, I hope to have eliminated one source of skepticism that the decline could be real: the intuition that the violent side of human nature makes it impossible. Not only have other declines of violence indisputably taken place over the course of human history, but such declines are fully compatible with an unsentimental appreciation of the crooked timber of humanity. A modern conception of human nature, rooted in cognitive science and evolutionary psychology, suggests that our species, however flawed, has the means to curb its own mean streak. Human nature is not a single trait or urge but a complex system comprising many parts, including several mechanisms that cause violence and several mechanisms that inhibit it. The mechanisms that cause violence, moreover, are not irresistible hydraulic forces but facultative reactions to particular circumstances, which can change over time. One of the mechanisms that inhibit violence is an open-ended combinatorial system capable of generating an infinite number of ideas. And, among those ideas are institutions that can lessen the probability of war.

Citations

Gaddis, John Lewis. (1989) *The Long Peace*. New York: Oxford University Press.

Gat, Azar. (2006) *War in Human Civilization*. Oxford: Oxford University Press.

Gleditsch, Nils Petter. (2008) "The Liberal Moment Fifteen Years On," *International Studies Quarterly* 52(4): 691–712.

Goldstein, Joshua S. (2011) *Winning the War on War*. New York: Dutton.

Holsti, Kalevi J. (1986) "The Horsemen of the Apocalypse,"
    International Studies Quarterly 30(4): 355–372.

Howard, Michael. (1991) *The Lessons of History*. New Haven, CT:
    Yale University Press.

Human Security Centre. (2005) *Human Security Report 2005*. New
    York: Oxford University Press.

Human Security Report Project. (2007) *Human Security Brief 2007*.
    Vancouver, BC: HSRP.

Human Security Report Project. (2011) *Human Security Report
    2009/2010*. New York: Human Security Report Project.

Jervis, Robert. (1988) "The Political Effects of Nuclear Weapons—A
    Comment," *International Security* 13(2): 80–90.

Keegan, John. (1993) *A History of Warfare*. New York: Vintage.

Lacina, Bethany, Nils Petter Gleditsch, and Bruce Russett. (2006)
    "The Declining Risk of Death in Battle," International Studies
    Quarterly 50(3): 673–680.

Long, William J., and Peter Brecke. (2003) *War and Reconciliation*.
    Cambridge, MA: MIT Press.

Luard, Evan. (1988) *The Blunted Sword*. New York: New Amsterdam
    Books.

Mueller, John. (1989) *Retreat from Doomsday*. New York: Basic Books.

Mueller, John. (2004) *The Remnants of War*. Ithaca, NY: Cornell
    University Press.

Mueller, John. (2009) "War Has Almost Ceased to Exist," *Political
    Science Quarterly* 124(2): 297–321.

Mueller, John. (2010) "Capitalism, Peace, and the Historical
    Movement of Ideas," *International Interactions* 36(2): 169–184

Payne, James L. (2004) *A History of Force*. Sandpoint, ID: Lytton
    52(4): 691–712.

Pinker, Steven. (2002) *The Blank Slate*. New York: Viking.

Pinker, Steven. (1994) *The Language Instinct*. New York:
    HarperCollins.

Pinker, Steven. (1997) *How the Mind Works*. New York: Norton.

Pinker, Steven. (1999) *Words and Rules*. New York: HarperCollins.

Pinker, Steven. (2011) *The Better Angels of Our Nature*. New York:
    Viking.

Ray, James L. (1989) "The Abolition of Slavery and the End of
    International War," *International Organization* 43(3): 405–439.

Russett, Bruce, and John Oneal. (2001) *Triangulating Peace*. New
    York: Norton.

3

THE ECONOMICS OF PEACE: HOW RICHER NEIGHBORS ARE VERY GOOD NEWS

By Emmanuel Martin

If one person gains, does someone else have to lose? Are the gains of one nation at the expense of others? Are human groups doomed to perpetual conflict? Emmanuel Martin is an economist and executive director of the Institute for Economic Studies–Europe. In addition to organizing programs across Europe and Africa, he was founding editor of UnMondeLibre.org and LibreAfrique. org. His writing has appeared in such publications as *Le Cercle des Échos* and *Les Échos* in France, *Il Foglio* in Italy, *L'Écho* in Belgium, *Libération* in Morocco, and *The Wall Street Journal–Europe*.

> *"War costs a nation more than its actual expense; it costs besides, all that would have been gained, but for its occurrence."*[24]
> —Jean-Baptiste Say

Winners and Losers
Many people believe that if one person profits, another has to lose. Such people believe that the sum of the benefits and the losses among persons is zero, meaning that for every gain for some, there

is a corresponding and equal loss for others. Accordingly, people who believe that, upon seeing someone prosper, look around to see who must have lost. If that were the only possible model of prosperity, social conflict would be omnipresent and war would be inevitable.

Fortunately, there are other modes of prospering that do not involve corresponding loss for others. The contemporary world is strong evidence of that, as incomes have gone up virtually everywhere in the world. More people live longer, healthier, and wealthier lives than in the past. Not only are more people prospering, but an ever-larger percentage of the world's population is doing so, as well.

In some cases, of course, the gain of one person does come at the expense of another. For example, if a thief steals something, the thief's gain comes at the expense of the victim. But gains can also come from activities other than stealing, such as work, innovation, discovery, investment, and exchange.

One of the most important economists of all times explained clearly and directly how your gain may be my gain, as well. In doing so, he explained not only the economic foundation for material prosperity, but for peace. Jean-Baptiste Say (1767–1832) is sometimes considered the "French Adam Smith," but in fact he was much more than merely a popularizer of Smith's insights. He advanced significantly on Smith's thought.

Like Smith, he was a critic of war, colonialism, slavery, and mercantilism and an advocate of peace, independence, liberation, and freedom of trade. He advanced beyond Smith not only in explaining that services have value (indeed, that the value of material goods is due to the services they render to us), but that the creation of goods and services is the source of the demand for other goods and services. That's sometimes called "Say's Law of Markets." It's a very important insight, not only for "macroeconomics," but for social relations generally, and for international relations in particular. If people are free to trade, the increasing wealth of one party is not harmful to, but is beneficial to the prosperity of their trading partners, for the increasing prosperity of one trading partner means that there is more effective demand for the goods and services of the others.

Enemies of free markets, notably economic nationalists and mercantilists, argue that if one country is becoming more prosperous, it must be at the expense of others. They have what is called a "zero-sum" view of the world, meaning that the sum of the gains is zero; if one person gains (a "plus"), someone else had to lose (a "minus"). Say showed that that is wrong. And that matters for peace, because it means that countries can prosper together, because there are mutual gains from voluntary trade. Trade is a "positive-sum" game, meaning that the sum of the gains is positive. In contrast, conflict and war are worse than zero-sum games, in which the gain of one party is equal to the loss of the other. Wars are almost invariably "negative-sum" games in which the sum of the losses are greater than any gains, and generally, in wars both parties lose.

A World of Producer-Consumers

> "Nations will be taught to know that they have really no interest in fighting one another; that they are sure to suffer all the calamities incident to defeat, while the advantages of success are altogether illusory."[25]   —Jean-Baptiste Say

Say explained that in an exchange economy humans should be seen as both producers and consumers. To produce is to "give value to things by giving them utility."[26] The progress of industry is measured by the ability to generate new products and to reduce the prices of already existing products. When more goods are produced, it means that the prices will be lower than they would be otherwise, which means that there is additional purchasing power leftover for the consumers to buy other goods.

Say explained that the entrepreneur is crucial in that process of "utility" creation. Say was an entrepreneur himself, and he understood the role of the "enterpriser," the one who "undertakes" new ventures and is looking for how to produce goods and services while sacrificing the least. (That's what it means to "cut costs" of production.) Say explained the important role of entrepreneurs in the market. Entrepreneurs have very often been portrayed as visionary geniuses who possess extraordinary abilities and comprehensive knowledge of markets, techniques, products, tastes, people, and so on. But Say explained that all of us, including the more "common" among us, also perform entrepreneurial activities.

One way to understand entrepreneurship is finding ways to produce at the least cost, which "frees up" scarce resources to be devoted to fulfilling other wants. The factory worker who sees how to produce the same amount with less time; the farmer who arranges the crops so as to minimize plowing and weeding time; the restaurateur who pays attention to when people leave work, so as to have the food ready at the right time; all are seeing how to increase production at the least cost. Arranging exchanges, too, is a form of production; it makes scarce products available in spaces or times where they would not otherwise be available and it increases the values of both parties to the transaction, which is why they exchange.[27]

"Say's Law" and Mutual Gains

A powerful theoretical construct that helps to understand economic development has become known as "Say's Law of Markets." In the chapter of his famous 1803 *Treatise on Political Economy* on *"Débouchés"* (the outlets for goods, which we could translate as "markets"), Say described how "it is production which opens a demand for products,"[28] because, as the idea was summed up later, "products are exchanged for products." The slogan "supply creates its own demand" that is frequently attributed to Say is a caricature of his insight. What Say was describing is precisely what we have seen as the world has become more and more prosperous, as the average wealth of the world has grown many times over since Say's time, as poverty has receded, and as health, literacy, longevity, and access to consumer goods have grown for the poor. He was one of the first to understand the mechanism of causation behind growing global prosperity, the "snowball effect" of rising wealth among trading partners. In the dry language of contemporary economics, it's an "inter-sectoral theory of economic growth" in which the growth of one producer/sector/nation represents a growing market or demand for other producers/sectors/nations. And when you think about it, that's really a cool thing to behold.

When traders produce more of their own specialized products, they generate more utility for others; those others, by specializing in production, also generate more utility that facilitates exchange; each has more "purchasing power" as he buys from the other. To use the vocabulary of another great French Economist, Jacques Rueff, each gains more "rights" by the utility he has created for the other. And more rights enable each to acquire more from the other.

Mutual gains in the context of exchange of products are cumulative. I get richer by providing my neighbor with more utility and my neighbor gets richer by providing more utility to me. And because I am richer I can buy more from my neighbor, who in turn will get richer. Obviously the possibilities for division of labor and production in a small or closed economy are limited, but in larger markets more possibilities open among numerous individuals, occupations, and industries. As Adam Smith explained before Say, "The division of labor is limited by the extent of the market."[29] Say added that "the more numerous are the producers, and the more various their productions, the more prompt, numerous, and extensive are the markets for those productions."[30]

Say described the positive sum game of exchange of products. In voluntary exchanges, the fact that my customers are getting richer is very good news for me. If, on the contrary, they become poorer, it's not good news at all, but bad news. In Say's words, "The success of one branch of commerce supplies more ample means of purchase, and consequently opens a market for the products of all the other branches; on the other hand, the stagnation of one channel of manufacture, or of commerce, is felt in all the rest."[31]

Say explained that economic development is a self-sustaining mechanism based (to use modern and rather dry language) on truly "endogenous growth": the "size of the market," which is so crucial to the level of specialization and division of labor, is endogenized in the sense that market size depends on production itself. More production generates more purchasing power, which translates into a larger market size, which in turn provides opportunities for more production.

The mechanism of development is obviously incremental and evolutionary, which is why in Say's time French people "bought and sold in France five or six times as many commodities, as in the miserable reign of Charles VI."[32] Division of labor and specialization increase the number of industries and create new branches of industry (and even branches of branches). A market economy is a process in constant motion.

Say was an optimist compared to most of his fellow economists at the time. Far from being obsessed by the idea of scarcity, he emphasized man's ability to create products and to generate wealth, and he explained how such production is a precondition for others to do the same; production and exchange are a positive sum game. For Say, scarcity was to be overcome by entrepreneurial spirit and services, by exchange and innovation. Thus for him, scarcity was not an obsession, as it was for Thomas Malthus, with whom Say debated. Say sought to study and understand the economics of prosperity and argued against Malthus's gloomy picture of humanity's future. Say turned out to be right, and Malthus turned out to be wrong.

Say's Law Applied at the International Level
Whether it is across borders or within them, to hurt one's neighbor is to hurt oneself: "Each individual is interested in the general prosperity of all, and . . . the success of one branch of industry promotes that of all the others."[33] Indeed, within a nation we very rarely find people complaining about the prosperity of another city or of another industry; most people understand that if French farmers are prospering, it will be good for French urban workers, and vice versa.

That is the true source of the gains made by the towns' people from exchange with the country people, and again by the latter with the former; both of them have wherewithal to buy more and better products, the more amply they themselves produce:

> A city, standing in the centre of a rich surrounding country, feels no want of rich and numerous customers; and, on the other hand, the vicinity of an opulent city gives additional value to the produce of the country. The division of nations into agricultural, manufacturing, and commercial, is idle enough. For the success of a people in agriculture is a stimulus to its manufacturing and commercial prosperity; and the

flourishing condition of its manufacture and commerce reflects a benefit upon its agriculture also.[34]

Say goes on to show how relations between countries are no different than relations between regions or cities and countrysides:

> The position of a nation, in respect of its neighbours, is analogous to the relation of one of its provinces to the others, or of the country to the town; it has an interest in their prosperity, being sure to profit by their opulence.[35]

Here again, rich neighbors mean an opportunity for us to sell more and become richer ourselves.

He makes his point even clearer in his correspondence with Malthus, and shows to what extent a merchant has an interest in the wealth of other countries or regions:

> When I advance that produce opens a vent for produce; that the means of industry, whatever they may be, when unshackled, always apply themselves to the objects most necessary to nations, and that these necessary objects create at once new populations and new enjoyments for those populations, all appearances are not against me. Let us only look back two hundred years, and suppose that a trader had carried a rich cargo to the places where New York and Philadelphia now stand; could he have sold it? Let us suppose even, that he had succeeded in founding there an agricultural or manufacturing establishment; could he have there sold a single article of his produce? No, undoubtedly. He must have consumed them himself. Why do we now see the contrary? Why is the merchandize carried to, or made at Philadelphia or New York, sure to be sold at the current price? It seems to me evident that it is because the cultivators, the traders, and now even the manufacturers of New York, Philadelphia, and the adjacent provinces, create, or send there, some productions, by means of which they purchase what is brought to them from other quarters.[36]

Trade Barriers ("Protectionism") as Negative-Sum Games

Many argued then, as some do today, that we don't need to trade with foreigners and that we should make everything "at home." Say offered a very insightful criticism of that mentality:

> Perhaps it will be said that "what is true with respect to a new state, may not be applicable to an old one: that there was in America room for new producers and new consumers; but in a country which already contains more producers than sufficient, additional consumers only are wanting." Permit me to answer, that the only true consumers are those who on their side produce, because they alone can buy the produce of others; and that unproductive consumers can buy nothing, unless by means of the value created by those who produce.[37]

Say describes how "protectionism" is self-destructive: it is as "if at the door of every house an import duty were laid upon coats and shoes, for the laudable purpose of compelling the inmates to make them for themselves."[38] In a very modern fashion, he was quite aware of the important role played by international value chains.

Some complain that some countries run "trade deficits" and others "trade surpluses," and even suggest that anything in "deficit" must be a bad thing. Say explained the fallacy of "the balance of trade," a destructive heritage from mercantilist thought that has been the cause of too many wars. "Trade wars" or "retaliations" are merely waged to protect the interests of a few who are cunning enough to make the public confuse their special interests with the interests of the entire nation.

Say was already wary of what we today call "Free Trade Agreements." Unilateral free trade was Say's favored policy: one should treat foreign nations as neighbors and friends. Exclusive commercial treaties entail unequal treatment of partners: "concessions" given to exporters from one nation mean "refusal of concessions" to others, and that is a source of conflict. Say could already perceive that instead of generating more trade, such treaties may merely generate "trade diversion," shifting trade flows away from nations whose governments were not parties to the treaty.

Say warned of the dangers of granting export subsidies. Such policies attract what are now called "cronies" or "rent seekers" who manipulate laws to their own benefit. Say was a critic of "crony capitalism" *avant la lettre*, or before it was more widely understood. Cronyism is merely, to use the term of another great French economist, Frédéric Bastiat: "mutual plunder."

An opponent of Say on free trade—and peace—was none other than Napoleon Bonaparte himself. While editor of the journal *Décade Philosophique*, Say had first supported Bonaparte's coup d'état in 1799 that ended the French Revolution and established the Consulat constitution. Say was actually even a member of the Tribunat, one of the four chambers of the Consulat. But after Say published his *Traité* in 1803, Bonaparte, who had become "Lifetime" Consul in 1802, insisted that Say should re-write sections on free trade and change them to support protectionism and government intervention. Say vehemently refused Bonaparte's request. His intellectual integrity caused him to be ousted from the Tribunat, to have the second edition of his *Traité* censored, and to be prohibited from working as a journalist.

Bonaparte became an opponent of Say on a very practical level, as well. After Say's expulsion from public life, he decided to launch a spinning company. Say was quite entrepreneurial, used the latest hydraulic engine, expanded the work force to 400 people, and offered serious competition to rival British producers. That was, until Bonaparte's protectionist policies ruined the company in 1812. Say and his company's workers and their families experienced directly the practical consequences of bad ideas.

Peace for Prosperity

Say lost his younger brother, Horace, a very promising intellectual, in 1799 during the French expedition to Egypt led by Bonaparte. Perhaps the loss of a younger brother in a colonial expedition helped Say to understand the full costs of war. In the later editions of the *Treatise*, Say was very critical of the "ruinous wars . . . such as occurred in France under the domination of Napoleon."[39]

Peace is the first condition of economic development. People do not invest or plan for the future as much when they are being massacred or threatened with massacre as they do when there is peace. Say stressed the importance of limiting plunder (or "spoliation") by government. Governments violate property not only when they can take away industries and lands, but also when they prescribe or prohibit certain usages of one's property. Say believed that governments should be limited and governed by rules (made "regular") and that "no nation has ever arrived at any degree of opulence that has not been subject to a regular government."[40]

Peace is obviously the first condition of mutual economic enrichment among nations. War destroys, cripples, and blights human lives, obliterates wealth, creates hunger, and wastes scarce resources. Wars are negative sum games. One of the tasks of political economy is to demonstrate their cost and the value of peace. Ask a Swiss in Zürich or a Swede in Stockholm today about the reasons for the marvelous wealth of either city or country; they will probably respond: "We did not blow ourselves up in two world wars." As Say put it:

> Nations will be taught to know that they have really no interest in fighting one another; that they are sure to suffer all the calamities incident to defeat, while the advantages of success are altogether illusory ... Dominion by land or sea will appear equally destitute of attraction, when it comes to be generally understood, that all its advantages rest with the rulers, and that the subjects at large derive no benefit whatever. To private individuals, the greatest possible benefit is entire freedom of intercourse, which can hardly be enjoyed except in peace. Nature prompts nations to mutual amity; and, if their governments take upon themselves to interrupt it, and engage them in hostility, they are equally inimical to their own people, and to those they war against. If their subjects are weak enough to second the ruinous vanity or ambition of their rulers in this propensity, I know not how to distinguish such egregious folly and absurdity, from that of the brutes that are trained to fight and tear each other to pieces, for the mere amusement of their savage masters.[41]

Peace and free trade reinforce each other to produce not only economic development, but genuine wealth and human flourishing.

4

INTERVIEW WITH A BUSINESSMAN FOR PEACE—CHRIS RUFER

By Tom G. Palmer

What's the connection between commerce and peace? What motivates a businessman to support peace and oppose foreign interventionism? What is the relationship between liberty, voluntary action, and peace? Chris Rufer founded the world's leading tomato ingredient processor and operates agriculturally based processing, distribution, and service enterprises. He is the founder of the Self-Management Institute and the Foundation for Harmony and Prosperity.

Palmer: Thanks for your time, Chris. Today, I actually did some business with you and your company, although I don't think you knew it. I bought some ketchup for my fries and had some tomatoes in my salad. From what I understand, there's a very good chance the tomatoes were processed by your company. So somehow the market connected us peacefully today. That leads to my first burning question: Why is a businessman so interested in the issue of peace?

Rufer: I suppose there are several ways to answer that. Peace allows us to transact business together, generating the highest shared value. So rather than being forced to do something one way or another, we can respond to each other's values, our true values. Peace is a prerequisite to voluntary exchange, which is what my business is all about. When we interact without force, on a voluntary basis, we learn about the values of our customers and our suppliers. And those customers, suppliers, and associates are the only ones who know their values. As a businessperson I respond to signals in the economy that tell me, in the form of prices, what is valued. That information comes to me as numbers, prices, that don't have nationalities or languages or races or religions tacked on. They're signals about the values of human beings.

That's one of the things that's so amazing about the market and about being in business. Prices have nothing else behind them; there are no prejudices; there's no nationality, no religion. They're the values of other people aggregated together and presented to me in the form of a price, which is expressed by a number that can be compared to other numbers. I can use those numbers to make decisions about allocating scarce resources. They tell me about the costs of resources, in the form of what others would pay to use them. Prices help me to become better attuned to the values of others.

Palmer: Do you do any international business?
Rufer: We do. In fact, about 30 percent of our product is sold internationally.

Palmer: To foreigners?
Rufer: To foreigners, but to me, they're just all customers. I don't worry about such things, except when governments get in the way. I'd say 10 percent to 20 percent of our sales are to folks in Canada and to folks in Mexico, but the other international sales are going all over the world. Every month we sell to customers in between forty and fifty countries—Japan, Saudi Arabia, the Netherlands, England, Argentina, just all over. Virtually all tomato paste and tomato products.

Palmer: And you make money on all of those sales?
Rufer: Well, sure, otherwise we don't make them. That tells me that we're adding value to the world, that we're responding to and fulfilling the values of our customers. It's got another effect, too, that's related to that responsiveness to the values of others. You can think of the

product you sell to another human being, whether it's across borders, (internationally) or within borders (domestically), as an emissary for peace, for cooperation, for respect. When you see other people as customers, it doesn't really occur to you to want to shoot them or hurt them. Trade is such a beautiful alternative to violence and coercion.

Palmer: Some people say that international trade causes environmental damage and harm and if . . .
Rufer: The businessperson, when working in a free market, which means with respect for the property rights of others, is the ultimate environmentalist. A real environmentalist sees the costs of goods, the costs of material resources, whether they be oil or wood or rubber or glass, or anything else. And because of the accounting made possible by prices, profit, and loss, the information about costs isn't just knowledge, it's effective knowledge; it changes behavior. Prices give us knowledge about costs and at the same time incentives to minimize them. We don't like to see things go to waste and we have incentives to make sure that doesn't happen. The key is respect for the rights of others, which means property; you get environmental degradation, pollution, waste, and destruction when property rights are not respected. When property rights are well defined and defended, we have to take into account the impact of our choices on others. You know, governments usually don't have to consider the impact of their actions on others, because they can resort to coercion, but we have to think about the values and rights of other people every minute of every day. Our business is centered on voluntary action. We can't and don't use force to make people consume our products, or produce them, or supply goods to us. It's all voluntary, right down the line.

Palmer: You've mentioned voluntary activity a lot. Do you describe yourself as a voluntaryist or a libertarian or . . . ?
Rufer: To me those terms are pretty similar. The old term was "liberal," but that sometimes causes a lot of confusion in the United States, because "liberal" is considered the opposite of "conservative" here. You could say I'm a "classical liberal," but with the right understanding of the terms, you might say I would subscribe to all

of them—liberal, classical liberal, voluntaryist, libertarian. What matters to me is that people are not coerced and that we interact voluntarily, peacefully.

Palmer: How long have you had those views, and how did you come to them?

Rufer: My parents were apolitical and I was very shy when I was a kid. Still am, I suppose. So I didn't engage in a lot of debate and whatnot. I never saw myself as an intellectual person. Then I went to UCLA as a freshman and lived in a dorm and was introduced to a lot of people my age, including a lot of folks a lot smarter than I am. That was really the first time I started talking about politics, and for some reason I seemed to argue a certain way, that I didn't think it was right to harm other people. And as time went on I just refined my arguments. It just seemed like commonsense to me. There may have been influences, but if so I didn't know where the influence came from. I can't recall a particular book or person or statement that caused me to believe the way I do. I tend to just look at things and try to understand how things work and how they could work better. At UCLA my major was economics and I had Tom Sowell as a labor professor and Armen Alchian and William Allen, who were also great teachers. The first class I went to was, I believe, Bill Allen's for Econ 1. So I suppose I was introduced to economics first. I've come to understand that economics is pretty important in understanding how people work.

Economics is a social science; it's not a division of mathematics as a lot of people try to make it today. It's a social science that studies how people coordinate with each other. I never got the idea that anyone was pushing any political agendas at all. I never heard the word "libertarian" back then, but I did start to think seriously about how people can coordinate their actions to achieve their values. And some time later I heard about libertarianism, and I just said, "That's me. That's basically what I think." There was no lightning flash of inspiration. I just thought that people should be able to live their lives peacefully and figure out how to achieve their values cooperatively. I only later learned that there was a name for my beliefs.

Palmer: So you were in college studying economics, which you saw as about voluntary cooperation. How did you go from studying it to practicing it in business? How did that happen?

Rufer: I grew up in a solid blue-collar family. But my grandfather was a small businessman, an entrepreneur. I remember going out to an oil field where he invested a little money in oil drilling. He had a patent or two and a workshop in his house. So he was a little bit of an inventor and an entrepreneur. I have memories of him from when I was very young. He died when I was about 12 years old. But I always had this vision that that's what it's like when you get older. Now, my father typically worked for my grandfather. Very much like on a farm. You're a little kid and you see your dad driving a tractor and your grandfather is going to the bank, doing the business transactions while your father is doing the operational kinds of things. I thought that was the path in life because I thought that everybody did that. It informed my life to some extent. I got a bachelor's degree in economics and a master's degree in agricultural sciences and later an MBA. I finished business school at UCLA and I never even interviewed for a job. I just moved up to Davis, California, and started advancing some of the ideas I had while I was driving a truck. So it was just part of my nature, part of my expectations.

I actually got into business in college. My dad supported me for about a year and a quarter. Then I was on my own. He just couldn't afford it anymore. There was no big discussion; I just pretty much absorbed that information and went out on my own and began working. My dad drove a truck most of the time through his life. So I figured I could drive a truck. So with some friends of his I picked up some ideas on hauling tomatoes from one place to another. When I was a junior in college—maybe a senior—I rented a truck and a set of trailers and worked under my father's license and got a job sub-hauling, hauling tomatoes and peaches and whatnot during the summer. Well, that went on five years, five summers.

Palmer: That was when you were in school?

Rufer: Yeah, so that got me through school and got me an introduction into business. In this case it was the tomato business. So as a trucker, you go out to the farm fields and grading stations and you go to the processing plants and you go look at the fruit. And so I just came up with some ideas. You know, "The system would work better if they just changed how they harvest the tomatoes and if the processors changed how they unloaded the tomatoes at the factory and moved the grading station from here to there. They could save a lot of wasted time and effort." I figured, "If this system changed a bit I could really make a lot of money as a trucker." So it all evolved out of my asking, "How could you do better?" I was looking into other people's businesses and trying to figure out how to improve the systems. So I designed a different system and presented it to some people. And I pounded the pavement and studied the processing industry more and came up with some ideas for designing a different tomato processing plant. I pushed that and tried to raise money for five years, pounding the pavement some more, and I finally raised enough money. And that was the time to build a factory. I had three big partners—I was the smallest partner—and we built our first tomato-paste processing factory. There were a few innovations in that factory and in the business that enabled us to do extremely well. Now, I was the smallest partner, but I took no salary and bargained for a larger percentage of the profits. In seven years I made my partners a lot of money and I made a lot of money. So it worked out really well. It was the right thing to do at the right time. I offered my partners a second plant, but they refused, so we parted ways. And I built another plant that I was able to finance all on my own. And it just went on from there.

Palmer: You promote a philosophy derived from your business experience that you call "self-management." You set up a Self-Management Institute to promote voluntary cooperation and self-management. How do you create win-win relationships, so that, as you put it in one of your videos on the institute's website, people's personal missions are compatible with or supportive of their commercial missions and vice versa?

Rufer: Self-management, to me, seems quite simple. In their personal lives people manage themselves. Nobody has a life boss.

They run their own lives. And they run their own lives based on having a mission. I believe that everybody's mission in life is to be happy. Whether they understand it or not, they're striving to be happy. Every organism strives to flourish. People have different ideas of what will make them happy. The key thing now in getting people to cooperate together voluntarily in business is to establish a mission for each person in the enterprise.

Human beings make subjective judgments about what will advance their purposes and when they exchange things, they haggle. They use their own subjective judgments and also the knowledge that they have, which others often don't have. So they exchange: so many of these for so many of those. Those ratios of exchange are turned into prices when people start to use money, which is the commodity that everyone will accept because they know others will accept it. The result is that their subjective judgments are translated into prices, which are expressed in terms of numbers, in the market economy. They're all expressed in terms of the same units, so they can be compared. How cool is that? You don't need a central planner to get coordination and order. That's the beautiful thing about the free market. And we work through self-management to bring the freedom and self-direction and benefits of a free-market economy into the company. People know things others don't but would find useful. Markets allow us to communicate while realizing our own subjective ends. We work to bring those principles into the company and we strive to rely on self-direction rather than hierarchies. And it yields superior results.

Palmer: Well, what about conflicts? Are they inevitable? Are conflicts just a constant, or are there ways to resolve them? What's your experience?
Rufer: Conflicts are inevitable. No question. You don't have economics if you don't have conflicts. There are limited resources and economics is the study of how to allocate limited resources. So there are going to be conflicts. Definitely. The issue is how best to resolve those conflicts. Conflict can be over human action or use of resources. There are two ways to resolve conflicts. You can discuss them and voluntarily agree on something, or one person

can use force against the other to resolve the conflict—peacefully or with force. If you can work with people who agree to resolve those conflicts peacefully, you win, everybody wins. I look for win-win resolutions of problems. Win-win resolutions create gains for all. They create peace. They create prosperity and happiness.

Palmer: Let's move to more political questions. Some people say they're pro-business. I hear other people say that they're pro-free market. Is there a difference between those two?

Rufer: The free market is voluntary action. When people talk about being pro-business, they may be talking about winning from a myopic perspective, you know, winning at the expense of the rights of others. Voluntary business is what is transacted under conditions of freedom, of free markets, with no special favors for this or that firm or group. If a business goes to government and uses it as an agent to get what it couldn't get voluntarily, that's flat out immoral and unproductive. Business should be voluntary, ethically operated, and not getting favors or subsidies at the expense of others through government coercion.

Unfortunately, and I really struggle against this, there's a kind of "market in favors," which means a market in coercion. It's like me using your gun to get what I want from someone else at gun point and then you and I share the loot. It's a kind of disease called "cronyism," which is what you get when government can use its powers to favor some groups at the expense of others. The cure is called the free market—freedom to compete, respect for everyone's rights, and equality before the law. Crony politics is simply going to the agency of government to use force. It's just like the mafia organizing shakedowns. No real difference.

Palmer: Let's go back to the issue of peace. What's the relationship between business and peace? You do business with people in Asia, Latin America, and the Middle East. Should businesspeople be supportive of peace?

Rufer: Absolutely. People in business should support peace in a number of ways. Number one is to incorporate peace into their values personally; I'm talking about within their enterprise, supporting peaceful solutions to problems and not going to government to ban competition or participating in crony politics. Don't take subsidies. Don't utilize government programs. Stay as far away as you can from coercive actors, meaning, basically, government agents.

Number two is to make ethical decisions not to trade in coercion, selling to governments the instruments of violence or coercion or oppression. It's important.

Number three is to promote peaceful connections among countries through voluntary trade. Trade decreases the chances of going to war. The more people get to know each other and to benefit each other through trade, the less chance there is of their governments going to war, because there are more people in both countries who will be for peace. The more trade there is, the more dependency A has on B and vice versa. I know there are a lot of studies on this, and economists and political scientists study peace and business and trade. I know it also from my experience of life and business. When customers are coming to your door, you don't want to shoot them. You want to welcome them in to benefit themselves *and* you *and* your family *and* your colleagues. You can trade or you can fight. I much, much prefer trading. It's civilized and it's better for everyone, except perhaps people who just like to hurt others. I'm not in that group.

Palmer: You talk about ethical decisions in business, but if you watch most TV shows, businesspeople are just bastards: they are not nice; they are not friendly; they are not ethical. They are just out to screw people. That's how most popular culture portrays the businessperson. How does ethics enter into business?

Rufer: One of the foundations of cooperation is friendship. If you do not have a friendship, how do you coordinate with other people in your productive life? You would be all alone. Now friendship can take a lot of forms. There are spouses and best friends and bowling friends and so on. There are also business friends, people you like being around because they treat you well and are helpful to you. People generally do not want to be around people that are nasty, let alone people who physically harm each other or steal from each other. So you can't have a civil relationship unless you respect those values of not harming people and not stealing. And beyond that, of course, people want to be around people who are pleasant.

So, if you want to have a business and you want it to be productive, and you want to have a larger business, you have very strong incentives to cooperate with others to gain their cooperation. I can think of only two ways to get people to do what you'd like: Number one, you can whip them or put a gun to their heads; I don't know of a person who likes having that done to him or her, so people tend to run from people who whip them and shoot them. Number two, you can respect them and their rights. In a free market, you have your choice about whom to do business with. To have a successful business you have to be a respectful and honorable person or other people will not want to associate with you. I could say more, but I am always puzzled by people who don't see the importance of ethics in business. It's like they aren't thinking.

Palmer: What about military intervention abroad by the government? How would you characterize that?
Rufer: I think it helps to think like the marketing department. What would other people like? Can you imagine having a Chinese, Russian, or even a Canadian army march through the cities of the United States? Just walking in their uniforms through Los Angeles or Denver? Or having military bases and driving military vehicles through town? Wow. That's what the US government is doing across the world. It has got to be abusive. It has got to tear down our reputation. Where they're actually defending the independence of the country, there's going to be good will built up. But when there is no clear issue like that, it's hard to see how our military presence is anything but a cause for hatred and resentment.

Palmer: You're an active supporter of libertarian values. How do you work to create a freer and more peaceful world?
Rufer: Everywhere I go I personally advocate for the values and principles of peace and liberty. In every nation I visit on business, there is not a luncheon, there is not a meeting, where I don't start some discussion on how society could be organized without coercion, without violence, and what we can do to help that. I'm outspoken.

Palmer: There is a long tradition of business leaders standing up for peace. I think about Richard Cobden and John Bright in England, who were both great business innovators and great peace leaders. The Anti-Imperialist League in the United States had many business people in it who opposed the Spanish-American War and the American occupation of the Philippines and other Spanish colonies. Do you see yourself as part of that tradition of business people for peace?

Rufer: I do. I know that businesspeople—not cronies, but honest businesspeople—are emissaries for peace. Voluntary exchange is a win-win deal all around. It's unfortunate that more people don't get that. There's an old saying I remember, "When goods cannot cross borders, armies will." I favor exchange of goods, rather than bullets and missiles. In the '60s people said, "Make Love, Not War." That's not bad, but I'd add, "Make Love and Business, Not War."

Palmer: What would you say to a young person who is thinking about what to do after school, whether high school or college, to make the world a better place? Would you recommend business? Or going into government?

Rufer: Going into government is a waste and I could expand on that. But I would certainly recommend going into business, as well as going into communications, be it journalism or some other kind of media.

Palmer: What about becoming a competitor in the tomato business?

Rufer: [Laughs] That would be fine. Going into business and getting involved with international trade, if you're interested in peace, would be a great thing. It actually makes the world a better place. And if anyone wants to get into business to compete with me, I'd welcome it. I wish there were some better competitors to keep me even more on my toes.

Palmer: Thanks for taking time from a very busy schedule, Chris.
Rufer: You bet.

5

THE FREE TRADE PEACE

By Erik Gartzke

> How do trade and cross-border investment reduce
> the incentives for war? How does interdependence af-
> fect behavior? What is the relationship between peace,
> democratically accountable government, and trade? Erik
> Gartzke is associate professor of political science at
> the University of California, San Diego, and professor
> of government at the University of Essex. His research
> focuses on the impact of information and institutions
> on war and peace. He publishes on trade, cyberwar,
> diplomacy, and related topics.

A series of brutal and destructive European wars lasting decades
was brought to an end in 1648, when the Peace of Westphalia, as it
came to be known, established a system in which European states
were sovereign within and autonomous without. That legacy is
increasingly challenged in a world where economic linkages cross
international borders. Economic interdependence is what results
when two or more nations are linked together by trade. The standard economic view is that trade creates value.

As students of politics have long noted, this value of trade is
then in effect held "hostage" in any conflict among nations. If the
hostage is sufficiently valuable and endangered by war, then sovereign states are no longer fully autonomous. Where the benefits
of trade are likely to be forfeited in the event of war, the mutual
prospect of loss can serve to deter conflict between trade partners.
Put more plainly, if people on one side of a border have assets or

valued customers on the other side, they are less likely to support destroying those assets or trade partnerships and more likely to raise their voices for peace.

Another important effect of trade in promoting peace and deterring war could be that it facilitates a fall in the valuation for the very goods likely to be obtained by fighting, while making occupying armies much more expensive. If trade lowers the real cost of goods and increases the productivity of labor, then workers, firms, and sovereign states should want to move labor toward productive enterprise and away from war. I examine these processes in more detail below, after reviewing some background information.

The Transformation

It doesn't take a PhD to see that the world we live in today is different in critical ways from what existed even a few generations ago, to say nothing of looking back to the seventeenth century. In particular, markets have begun to do for world affairs what they have already done to the politics *within* nations in so many places. Gradually at first, but at an increasing pace in recent decades, world leaders have begun to discover that their countries and populations are bound together by complex and extensive economic networks. Figure 1 provides a simple illustration of this evolution in terms of global trade, measured as real 2000 US dollars (in hundreds of billions).

The world is also becoming more prosperous, on average. Figure 2 shows world GDP per capita. To make comparisons across time easier, I rescale values so that average income in 1821 is equal to one. That also allows for a comparison of rising wealth with the march toward more limited government and personal freedom. While global democratization appears more uneven—in large part this is because decolonization dramatically increased the number of countries after 1950—this is also on an upward trend, a phenomenon well documented as "waves" of political reform.[42] Polity data measure national democracy levels where ten is the highest and zero lowest.[43] Here, both polity and GDP per capita are represented as annual world average levels.[44]

Figure 1

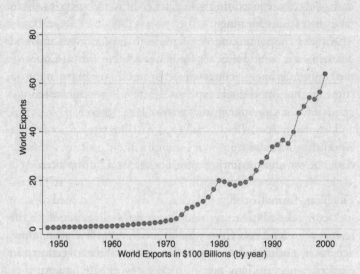

Figure 2

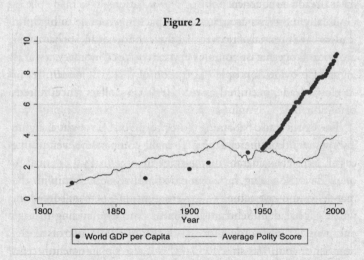

Classical liberal political economy anticipated all three of these changes and speculated about their consequences. Democracy, trade, and economic development all improve the human condition in a number of ways. The focus here is on whether, how, and which change discourages the use of political violence (within) and warfare (between) the existing system of Westphalian nations. Trade is an especially appealing tool for promoting world peace, but its effects are also complicated because of how it functions and what trade does to alter political competition and conflict. Countries tied together through common commercial bonds may in fact be "roped in" to peaceful relations. My goal is to try to make sense of the effects of economic interdependence.

Doubting Thomas

One of the most compelling descriptions of how interdependence works comes from Nobel Prize winning economist Thomas Schelling.[45] Schelling offers a parable of two climbers roped together to ascend a mountain. By binding themselves to each other, the climbers' fates become entwined and their actions become mutually dependent. Since the two climbers must climb or fall together, each becomes more cautious, acts with greater discretion, and produces peace as a consequence.

Liberal theorists use the logic of interdependence to highlight the pacific potential of trade. As international commerce has grown irregularly but persistently since the seventeenth century, a stream of scholars from Montesquieu, Smith, Paine, Kant, Cobden, Angell, and others to contemporary thinkers such as Rosecrance, Russett, and Doyle have emphasized the pacifying power of profitable cross-border trade.[46] Nations will be less likely to fight if linked by profitable commercial relationships, which in the event of war would cause considerable economic loss.

It is worth noting, however, that Schelling's interest in interdependence did not actually stem from trade, but from something quite different. In Schelling's parable, the rope binding the two mountain climbers together is not trade but the risk of nuclear war. The Cold War stalemate centered on a phenomenon colorfully labeled MAD, or Mutual Assured Destruction. The advent of nuclear weapons and the reciprocal risk of annihilation in a "shooting war" ensured that both the United States and the Soviet Union were deterred by the other, even as neither nation could protect themselves. Just like the two mountain climbers, cooperation and restraint evolved from the egoist desire to avoid destruction, not from an altruistic objective of promoting peace.

At the same time, Schelling's objective for the illustration was not to explain stability but to decipher ways in which the superpowers could *continue to compete* in a world in which direct and overt confrontation appeared unthinkable or at least irrational. As the parable makes clear, bonds of mutual dependence—whether nuclear or economic—can deter aggression. Yet, even as nuclear interdependence produced a world in which total war would not occur, it also produced an environment where *brinkmanship, coercive diplomacy, propaganda, and proxy conflicts* and other forms of threshold conflict proliferated. Fear of the consequences of failing to come to an agreement, whatever the sources of this fear, can force interdependent actors to compromise, but inhibitions produced by interdependence also encourage actors to play a game called "chicken."

Trade has little in common with nuclear weapons; one is something we seek to promote while the other is something humanity would rather eradicate. However, the roles of those two processes in making the actions of states mutually dependent are in important ways essentially the same. Both involve "selfish" behavior that may have virtuous social consequences, not unlike the virtuous social dynamic that Smith discovered hidden within the market mechanism.

As liberal theorists have long argued, rising quantities of trade create more intensive "hostages" and thus increase the incentives for peace; higher levels of interdependence occurring today may help to make war too costly for states to contemplate. Yet, the value of trade ties is typically far less substantial than the stakes in nuclear war. If nations are already willing to risk enormous losses in conducting conventional or nuclear combat, what more can commerce do to stem the tide of war? What then is the role of economic interdependence in promoting peace?

The Causes of Peace

One of the most remarkable events in world history is taking place right now. In fact, it has been ongoing for an extended period of time. A long-term "secular" decline in conflict has occurred among rich, prosperous countries. Peace has broken out, at least in some parts of the globe. This trend is so subtle, in fact, that many have missed it, even as others seem to prefer to ignore good news in favor of evidence that nations and groups are still fighting somewhere. The downward trend in war has been extensively chronicled by Steven Pinker, Joshua Goldstein, and others.[47]

The secular decline in war is most noticeable in Europe, where the trend has established itself over centuries. Figure 3, titled "Trend in Conflicts in Europe," is based on data collected by Peter Brecke.[48] Each small square represents the number of conflicts per decade (a conflict equals a minimum of thirty-two conflict-related fatalities). Conflicts in Europe have decreased over time from an average of thirty per decade in the 1400s to roughly ten per decade in the last century. Care should of course be taken in interpreting any relationship drawn from data where relationships are likely to be complex and multi-causal. For example, Claudio Cioffi-Revilla has shown that the intensity of conflicts in terms of casualties trends in the opposite direction, rising over time.[49] Still, the trend seems clear; over a long period of time European sovereigns have been shifting away from conflict and toward non-violent methods of resolving their differences.

A similar, if slightly more equivocal relationship, also appears at the global level. Figure 4 details annual incidents of Militarized Interstate Disputes, events as small as a threat to use force and as large as an occasional war. These data are again aggregated at the global level, meaning that MIDs have been weighted by the number of pairs of countries in the system in a given year. While no clear pattern arises until after World War II, militarized disputes seem to become less common in the aftermath of the two world wars. Again, the world is becoming more peaceful.

Figure 3

Trend in Conflicts in Europe

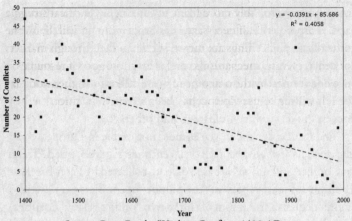

Source: Peter Brecke "Violent Conflicts 1400 AD to
the Present in Different Regions of the World."

What explains that trend? There are many possibilities. A number of scholars point to the rise of democracy as an important cause of interstate peace. While there is evidence to support this, there are problems with attributing peace to peaceful domestic politics.[50] To begin with, the rise of democracy in Europe is much later than the beginning of the downward trend in warfare. Democracy cannot cause peace until there are democracies. Taken a step further, democracy itself is the product of peace. A necessary condition for democracy is that groups within a society consider losing politically to be preferable to escalating their disputes to the level of violence. Contestation may well be muted by the choice of political institutions. However, a simpler and equally plausible claim is that the choice of political institutions itself depends on the nature of contestation. If what is being contested is so important that one cannot afford to compromise, then democracy may well fail. A prior condition for democracy is thus a level of consensus or moderation about what choices will prevail. If losing a political issue is not worth resorting to violence domestically, then it will be possible, even appealing, for elites and citizens to adopt popular rule and limited government in their domestic institutions. One way to enable this is for politics, or "public choice," to play less of a role in allocating resources or assets. If losing a political contest means losing your house, your business, your freedom, or even your life, then you are probably more likely to continue a political struggle and to use violence, if necessary, in an attempt to prevail. If, on the other hand, such things are increasingly handled through markets or other, private, mechanisms and when allocation of resources is not determined by the outcome of political contests, then you may be less willing to use violence in order to win in politics.

Figure 4

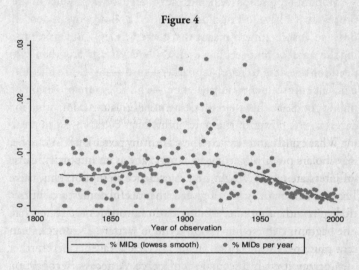

Militarized Interstate Disputes (MIDs)

In pre-modern societies, the means of production were mostly tangible. People owned land and labor that could be appropriated by sovereigns for their own ends. Being wealthy—or even being allowed to live—meant being in the good graces of the king. As societies developed, wealth increasingly became a function of knowledge and the ability to think creatively. The king could still choose winners, but the productivity of the society depended increasingly on choosing winners that were smart and effective commercially, something that markets did best when not dependent on the king. It was this new kind of commercial independence from politics that made it in the interest of the sovereign to limit his (or occasionally her) intrusions into markets in order to allow his or her economy to grow and for the society (and the state) to prosper. The growth of civil society and independent enterprise meant that wealth was no longer a function of loyalty to the king or proximity to the state. Security in turn could be had by being so productive that the sovereign would not intervene or plunder, rather than by ingratiating oneself to monarchs.[51] Even kings and queens came to understand the valuable lesson of the goose with golden eggs.

Modern representative democracy is arguably a product of the process that I have just outlined; the need to limit government in order to ensure growth meant that there was less value in capturing the state for rent-seeking, even as there was a greater than ever need for the state to regulate markets—providing clear rules and efficient enforcement (transparency)—and to ensure provision of public goods. Rather than investing in politics and competing for access to the power of the state, individuals could invest in creating more goods and services for sale through markets. Moreover, if it was not worth fighting to capture the state internally, there was also less reason to fight over tangible property internationally. The rise of democracy as a global phenomenon may well *reflect* the declining importance of distributional politics in Europe and elsewhere, as depicted in Figure 1, rather than explaining the pattern observed in the figure.

Commerce could discourage conflict in several ways. Recognition of the role of trade in helping to make world politics more peaceful is fairly widespread and well established among academics.[52] Yet, the precise mechanism and how it can be nurtured and propagated remains a subject of controversy. As I have suggested, having something to lose is not itself a barrier to fighting, and may well promote conflict when someone else is interested in appropriating one's wealth. Merely having something to lose often increases conflict if competition is zero-sum (my welfare depends on your defeat and vise versa) as is often the case in politics. Since politics is itself a struggle, we must look to how trade, and commerce more generally, tie politics to peace.

The "Invisible Hand" of Peace

One of the great insights of social science is Adam Smith's recognition that actions can have unintended consequences and that the social value of those consequences need not follow from the intentions of the actors. Markets have virtuous effects on communities and nations, even when participants in a market are only acting with the intention of improving their own welfare. A similar argument can be made about the effects of markets on peace. By simply attempting to get rich, firms, consumers, entrepreneurs, and even states have altered the utility and in some cases the viability of military force. The invisible hand in this case is more a set of hands. Markets make labor expensive, reducing the appeal of using labor to appropriate capital. Markets also facilitate the transfer of goods and services through peaceful means. Finally, markets themselves do not respond well to conflict, providing an incentive to suppress violence.

The most potent effect of commerce on conflict may be in transforming state interests. The growing depth and integration of markets has increased the value of labor and of "human capital" (e.g., skills) enormously over the centuries.[53] Expensive labor and the declining value of tangible inputs to production appear to have led many nations to abandon once-common attempts to "steal" prosperity by plundering the assets of other nations. One must be careful, of course, as the narrow interests of rulers and their key supporters can overpower the public interest and encourage predation, either within or between states.

Ancient empires prospered by demanding tribute (shiploads of grain and other goods) from subject provinces. Viking raiders loaded their ships with plundered loot. Spanish galleons in the sixteenth century brought home shiploads of silver bullion mined and refined by enslaved native populations. Later European imperial states, on the other hand, often fleeced their own citizens to subsidize foreign adventures that were profitable only to the second scions of the aristocracy. As historians Lance E. Davis and Robert A. Huttenback concluded, "The British as a whole certainly did not benefit economically from the Empire. On the other hand, individual investors did."[54] Even colonialism declined as modernity prompted the most prosperous and militarily capable nations to prefer to purchase inputs to production, rather than appropriating them through an increasingly expensive exercise of arms. Modern nations no longer consider it profitable to raid their neighbors, as did Vikings, conquistadors, and Elizabethan sailors. Subduing foreign populations to extract resources and the fruits of human labor makes much less sense when paying the occupiers is expensive and as it becomes cheaper to buy what one wants, rather than plundering one's neighbor to get it.

Ironically, while there is no longer much benefit to modern nations from plunder—a reality made stronger by the increasing liquidity of global markets—commerce has increased the benefits of policing the global commons, i.e., reducing the general incidence of violence. Modern nations take more, rather than less, interest in the politics and policies of other nations, precisely because interdependence ensures that what others do has more impact on one's own well-being. International troops, rather than conquering and looting armies, are increasingly deployed on behalf of the United Nations or regional groups as "peacekeeping" forces charged with stopping or reducing violent conflict. Peace may be imposed externally so that commerce can continue, at least when the nations involved are fragile and when localized political agendas interfere in world affairs. Put another way, trade among the richest ensures that powerful nations have an incentive to discourage *other* nations from engaging in conflict, because fighting harms trade ecologically, not just among the nations that are fighting, and because powerful beneficiaries of trade have incentives to discourage disruptions of trade caused by conflict among third parties.

One of the challenges of an interdependent world is its very complexity. Simple relationships have the advantage that they are easier to understand and they may perhaps appear easier to address through effective policies. At the same time, complexity can be a virtue where it increases options, offering a broader set of responses, with more alternatives to military force. Trade can lead to peace if it constrains nations from fighting, but that requires really big trade relationships that are so valuable that they deter (like nuclear weapons). It may also require a set of issues or disputes that are relatively modest in scope, such as has occurred for example in Western Europe in the aftermath of World War II. Where trade is extremely valuable and states do not much disagree, peace should prevail. Trade can also inform disputants, allowing nations to resolve differences through diplomatic bargains, rather than requiring the use of military force to demonstrate resolve in an uncertain and fractious environment. Finally, perhaps the most general effect of trade is that it transforms the objective interests of nations, ensuring that the old logic of predation is increasingly recognized to be anachronistic. Even bank robbers buy their groceries, rather than stealing from the local shop. It is simply not worth the effort to steal much of what could be plundered today, even as much of what is worth stealing cannot be plundered. Rising trade promotes specialization which makes predation less effective and increases the benefits of peace. Skilled workers must be enticed with good working conditions, which makes war and conquest counter-productive. Increasingly, modernity means we buy rather than steal.

By tying nations together and making the world more interdependent, market forces have shaped what it is that nations seek, making war a less effective tool for fulfilling national objectives, just as leaders and populations find ownership of the state less critical for their own survival. At the same time, the role of the state in facilitating market conditions is ever more important. States work not just internally but regionally and internationally to facilitate trade, increasing interdependence in a chain of causation that reinforces cooperation and further limits conflict. It's not merely that people have tried to do more good, but that trade has changed what it means to do well. If we are fortunate and continue along the path toward broader and freer trade, then trade will continue to make military force increasingly futile or inefficient.

6

THE POLITICAL ECONOMY OF EMPIRE AND WAR

By Tom G. Palmer

Do civilizations have to clash? Is imperialism or colonialism a winning—or a losing—proposition? Who were the greatest champions of peace and opponents of colonialism? Must there be "wars for oil"? Who decides on issues of war and peace and who gains?

"Liberty within, peace without. This is the entire plan."[55]
—Frédéric Bastiat (1849)

Some people study war to become better at it. We can also study war—from a different perspective—to avoid war, to reduce war, to stop war, to eliminate war. We can seek to understand war, not as we understand the weather or astronomy or even disease, but as we understand other kinds of human behavior. Equipped with such understanding, we can enlighten ourselves and our neighbors, friends, families, and fellow citizens about the fallacies underlying specious justifications for wars. Moreover, we can work to institute and strengthen those institutions that make war less likely. If we come to understand the issues involved better, we can reduce the occasions for wars and reduce the human experience of violence. Misinformation and misunderstanding can—quite literally—be deadly. Information and understanding can save lives.

Libertarian thinkers have devoted a great deal of their energies over the last few centuries to understanding the causes of wars and to fostering the mentalities and the institutions that make peace more likely.

Peace is no longer merely a utopian fantasy. In fact, the historical record shows that the world has become more peaceful. And the sciences of economics, sociology, and psychology explain why. Armed (so to speak) with that knowledge, we can make the world far more peaceful. We can reduce the human experience of violence. The world can be simultaneously more peaceful, more just, more prosperous, and more free.

The Good News: Violence Is Declining

"Believe it or not—and I know that most people do not—violence has declined over long stretches of time, and today we may be living in the most peaceable era in our species' existence."[56]   —Steven Pinker

If someone says that violence is going down, most people quickly deny it. After all, the news is full of stories about violence, often accompanied by gory images. Rapes and murders and assaults are staples of the nightly news. "If it bleeds, it leads." One country or another is mired in armed conflict. But we need to take a step back to get the bigger picture. Conflict, especially violent and deadly conflict, is far more attention-grabbing than peaceful cooperation. When there is peaceful and voluntary interaction, we're accustomed to saying that "nothing happened," but in fact lots of things happened: people went to work, farmers planted crops, investors financed new companies, and factory workers assembled useful products; people shopped; people fell in love; lovers got married; babies were born; there were birthday parties; *life* happened. But that's the background. It's normal. No headline ever read "Billions Went About Their Business Peacefully." What merits a headline is what's abnormal and more often than not, that's conflict, especially violence. In fact, and it may seem paradoxical, the *less common* violence is, the *more likely* it is to be covered. We deceive ourselves into thinking that the world is becoming more violent when it's becoming less so.

Political scientist James Payne and psychologist Steven Pinker have documented something remarkable.[57] The likelihood that a person chosen at random will be subjected to violence has generally fallen over thousands of years. Even counting the unspeakable horrors of the first and second world wars, the slave-labor camps of the Third Reich, the USSR, and the People's Republic of China, the "ethnic cleansings" and other horrors of the past one hundred years, the experience of violence in people's day-to-day lives has been falling. It doesn't seem possible, but it is the case. So there are abundant reasons to be encouraged, even as our hearts are broken by the fates of those still subject to violence. The good news is that it's a less and less common experience and has been becoming less common for quite a long time.

Violence, including war, is not an invariant feature of human nature. Its incidence has declined over time. We are not doomed to suffer from a constant quantity of violence in the world. Violence waxes and it wanes; for a very long time it has been waning. The social and political sciences help us to understand why. Scholars have accumulated and tested a great deal of evidence showing that classical liberals of the past were right in maintaining that the key to securing peace is liberty, notably the freedom to question and criticize governments and the freedom to trade, travel, and invest abroad.

Do Civilizations or Countries Have to "Clash"?

There is a famous thesis according to which the world is facing a "clash of civilizations." According to the political scientist Samuel Huntington, "the West" is in decline because, among other things, "Western countries" control less of the surface of the planet militarily. In Huntington's view, the interests of "civilizations" are at odds, and if one rises, others must fall.

Huntington offers many interesting insights in his book, but he had a poor understanding of the political economy of human interactions. His grasp of economics was weak and he failed to comprehend the importance of voluntary trade, which is a feature common to civilizations and the means by which they enrich each other. He subscribed, instead, to a zero-sum view of social relations.[58]

Here, for example, is one of the primary ways he measures the "decline" of a civilization.

> In 1490 Western societies controlled most of the European peninsula outside the Balkans or perhaps 1.5 million square miles out of a global land area (apart from Antarctica) of 52.5 million square miles. At the peak of its territorial expansion in 1920, the West directly ruled about 25.5 million square miles or close to half the earth's earth. By 1993 this territorial control had been cut in half to about 12.7 million square miles. The West was back to its original European core plus its spacious settler-populated lands in North America, Australia, and New Zealand. The territory of independent Islamic societies, in contrast, rose from 1.9 million square miles in 1920 to over 11 million square miles in 1993. Similar changes occurred in the control of population. In 1900 Westerners composed roughly 30 percent of the world's population and Western governments ruled almost 45 percent of the population then and 48 percent in 1920. In 1993, except for a few small imperial remnants like Hong Kong, Western governments ruled no one but Westerners.[59]

Is that a decline? Let's look into the case of just one of those Western countries and its empire. The Kingdom of the Netherlands had ruled over what was to become Indonesia from 1800 to 1942, when the region was conquered by the Empire of Japan. The Dutch government returned after the war and struggled for almost five years to reestablish Dutch colonial control. They failed and Indonesia became an independent country in 1950.

Naturally, after that loss, one would expect, following Huntington's thesis, that the fortunes of Dutch people were waning. Were they? Using the purchasing power of the US dollar in 1990 as the standard of income, in 1950 per capita GDP in the Netherlands (the amount of income per person in the Netherlands) stood at

US$5,996.[60] What was it in 2010? The per capita GDP of the Netherlands in 2010, measured in 1990 US dollars, stood at US$24,303, representing an increase of 305 percent.[61] The "loss" of the Dutch East Indies as a colonial possession of the Dutch government was no disaster for the Dutch people. Far from it. They no longer send their young men to fight and swarms of bureaucrats to administer. Now, when Dutch people want something from Indonesia, they can buy it, without having to spill their blood and treasure on the soil of another country. It turns out that trade, rather than imperialism, is a great deal more advantageous for the Dutch and far more advantageous for the Indonesians, as well, whose per capita GDP (measured, again, in constant 1990 US dollars) went from $817 in 1950 to $4,722 in 2010, representing an increase of 478 percent.[62]

In fact, there is no necessity that one nation's prosperity must mean another's poverty. When your trading partner becomes more prosperous, it's good for you. As the economist Jean-Baptiste Say explained in 1803 (but too few were listening),

> a good harvest is favourable, not only to the agriculturist, but likewise to the dealers in all commodities generally. The greater the crop, the larger are the purchases of the growers. A bad harvest, on the contrary, hurts the sale of commodities at large. And so it is also with the products of manufacture and commerce. The success of one branch of commerce supplies more ample means of purchase, and consequently opens a market for the products of all the other branches; on the other hand, the stagnation of one channel of manufacture, or of commerce, is felt in all the rest.[63]

Economic nationalists in wealthy nations shake their fists when they read that Chinese or Indian or Brazilian or Ghanaian people are becoming richer. After all, if the poorer are becoming richer, it must mean that the richer are becoming poorer! But that's not only ugly and mean-spirited; it's based on bad reasoning. Canadians (or Germans or Danes or Americans or Japanese or anyone else) should not become angry if Chinese or Indians become wealthier; if they are trading with them, it's to the benefit of those people that their customers can pay more for their products. And the same goes for Koreans and Kenyans, Virginians and Vermonters, farmers and factory workers.

If all economic interactions were zero-sum interactions, it would mean that the interests of nations would be irreconcilably opposed. And if that were the case, conflict would be inevitable. Huntington would be right. But he was wrong.[64]

Is Mercantilist Imperialism a Winning Proposition?

Although a few rare voices were raised against war and empire throughout the ages, invading other countries, enslaving the local population, and confiscating their goods were not, sadly enough, widely condemned. It was the rising awareness of the benefits of trade based on respect for individual rights and the harm to self occasioned by the injustice of violence that provided the foundation for a principled criticism of invasion and conquest. It should be no surprise that the moral philosopher who published *The Theory of Moral Sentiments* in 1759 would later condemn the "folly and injustice" of European colonization in his book of 1776:

> Folly and injustice seem to have been the principles which presided over and directed the first project of establishing those colonies; the folly of hunting after gold and silver mines, and the injustice of coveting the possession of a country whose harmless natives, far from having ever injured the people of Europe, had received the first adventurers with every mark of kindness and hospitality.[65]

Adam Smith realized that imperialism "doesn't pay," at least for the majority of the people, and that the full costs of empires are far, far, far greater than the sum of any benefits they might reap. The Scottish moral philosopher and economist noted that, in addition to the injustices occasioned, such military adventures and empires cost far more to the taxpayers than the sum of all the possible benefits.

> A great empire has been established for the sole purpose of raising up a nation of customers who should be obliged to

buy from the shops of our different producers, all the goods with which these could supply them. For the sake of that little enhancement of price which this monopoly might afford our producers, the home-consumers have been burdened with the whole expense of maintaining and defending that empire. For this purpose, and for this purpose only, in the two last wars, more than two hundred millions have been spent, and a new debt of more than a hundred and seventy millions has been contracted over and above all that had been expended for the same purpose in former wars. The interest of this debt alone is not only greater than the whole extraordinary profit, which, it ever could be pretended, was made by the monopoly of the colony trade, but than the whole value of that trade or than that whole value of the goods, which at an average have been annually exported to the colonies.[66]

Colonialism and imperialism and the wars of conquest and subjugation they entailed were *not*, in fact, to the benefit of the populations of the colonizing countries, that is, to the people who paid the taxes, supplied the armies, and bore the burdens of empire. There were beneficiaries, to be sure: the war contractors and suppliers, the bureaucratic administrators and viceroys, the recipients of trade monopolies and stolen land, the traffickers in looted goods and in forced labor. But their gains were miniscule compared to the losses imposed on the suffering taxpayers of the colonizing country and the conquered inhabitants of the colonies. As Adam Smith noted, merely the interest on the debt required to finance the military forces involved was greater than the value of the trade involved. Taken altogether, it was a losing proposition.[67]

That was well understood by the classical liberal free traders. In 1860 Richard Cobden, a member of the British parliament and one of the most prominent and outspoken free traders in European history, noted acidly that if one simply wanted to subsidize powerful special interests, there were far cheaper and less harmful ways of doing so. He was famous for having negotiated a free trade agreement with France, which helped to secure a lasting peace between the two traditional adversaries. In a commentary on the folly of the British Empire, he playfully suggested a rather different and less destructive and costly approach to satisfying the predatory parties involved. It would be far better simply to deliver to the war profiteers, at a small fraction of the cost of war, wealth equal to what they would have received from war and empire, and to spare the rest of society the burden of fighting and dying:

> Unfortunately, we have a class—and that the most influential one—which makes money out of these distant wars, or these home panics about a French invasion. How could your aristocracy endure without this expenditure for wars and armaments? Could not a less worthy and inhuman method of supporting them be hit upon? When I am talking over the reduction of duties with M. Rouher, and we come to some small industry employing a few hands and a little capital, which has put in its claim for high protection, I am in the habit of suggesting to him that rather than interfere with the trade of the country for the purpose of feeding and clothing these small protected interests, he had better withdraw the parties from their unprofitable occupations, take some handsome apartments for them in the Louvre Hotel, and feast them on venison and champagne at the country's expense for the rest of their days. Might not a similar compromise be entered into with the younger sons of our aristocracy, instead of supporting them by the most costly of all processes, that of war or preparation for war?[68]

John Bright, also a founder of the free-trade movement in Britain and, like Cobden, an anti-imperialist member of Parliament, in 1858 compared the British Empire and its wars with a system of welfare payments ("out-door relief") to the rich.

> There is no actuary in existence who can calculate how much of the wealth, of the strength, of the supremacy of the territorial families of England has been derived from an unholy participation in the fruits of the industry of the people, which have been wrested from them by every device of taxation, and

squandered in every conceivable crime of which a Government could possibly be guilty. The more you examine this matter the more you will come to the conclusion which I have arrived at, that this foreign policy, this regard for "the liberties of Europe," this care at one time for "the Protestant interests," this excessive love for the "balance of power," is neither more nor less than a gigantic system of out-door relief for the aristocracy of Great Britain.[69]

Some Britons, for example, providers of services to the military and even "the younger sons of the aristocracy" who sailed off to be colonial governors or military officers, were gainers at the expense of both the colonized and the rest of the population of Great Britain. But the British people as a whole certainly did not benefit. Quite the contrary. After a serious study of the expenditures, investments, taxes, and other finances of the British Empire, Lance E. Davis and Robert A. Huttenback in their study *Mammon and the Pursuit of Empire: The Economics of British Imperialism,* concluded that

the British as a whole certainly did not benefit economically from the Empire. On the other hand, individual investors did. In the Empire itself, the level of benefits depended upon whom one asked and how one calculated. For the colonies of white settlement the answer is unambiguous: They paid for little and received a great deal. In the dependent Empire the white settlers, such as there were, almost certainly gained as well. As far as the indigenous population was concerned, while they received a market basket of government commodities at truly wholesale prices, there is no evidence to suggest that, had they been given a free choice, they would have bought the particular commodities offered, even at the bargain-basement rates.[70]

Imperialism is not to the economic advantage of the population of the colonial power as a whole, although it must be to the advantage of some subsection of them, or it would not be pursued. Those who benefit are a very small minority of the population and their gains are tiny in comparison to the losses suffered by others. The naïve assumptions of too many, both on the left and on the right, are that "if someone gains, someone else must have lost;" "if someone lost, someone else had to gain;" and "gains and losses always balance." Those assumptions are false.

We are surrounded by what social scientists call positive-sum games and most people call win-win deals, in which both parties to transactions benefit. When a customer buys something from a merchant, the customer says "thank you." A person who believes that the world is zero-sum should be surprised to hear both the merchant and the customer say "thank you." One is not suffering a loss to do a favor to the other. The gain of one is not balanced by the loss of the other. Instead, they both gain. The sum of the benefits is not zero, but positive. Such transactions are all around us, but few people ever notice the "double thank you" of positive-sum voluntary exchanges.

There is yet another kind of interaction, known as a negative-sum game. It's also possible in cases of conflict not merely for one party to lose, but for the losses to greatly outweigh the gains, and even for both parties to be losers. Indeed, the latter is quite common. (To be clear, it should be noted that a negative-sum game can include net gainers. A thief who stabs someone to death to take his or her money may get $10, but the victim loses not merely $10, but his or her life. One gains a little by imposing a complete loss on the loser. It may also be the case that both lose, if, for example, they fight and are both killed, or both are seriously wounded, all in a conflict over the $10 that the thief had hoped to steal.)

Viking raids once netted shiploads of loot for the raiders. The Spanish Silver Fleet brought precious metals—dug by slave labor from the earth—to Spain from royal colonies; that at least enriched the court (although it proved disastrous for the country as a whole). Pirates were once a huge threat to people risking the seas. But the world changed. In the case of the foreign military adventures of the past two centuries, the harms imposed on colonized people did *not* result in gains to the populations—taken as a whole—of the countries whose states were involved in imperial adventures. There were certainly net gainers (the special interests who provided the military its supplies, for example), but the gains were far less than the losses, not only to the colonized or occupied, but to the people of the occupying power, as well. And in the case of general wars, such as World Wars I and II, the losses to all sides were staggering. At the end of World War II, Europe and much of Asia were in ruins and populations across the two continents were suffering food rationing or even starvation. Peace and commerce, not war, provided the ground for the post-war economic recoveries.[71]

The most resolute opponents of imperialism and of military adventures overseas, whether in France, England, or Germany, were the most dedicated free traders. The first winner of the Nobel Peace Prize, Frédéric Passy, was a leading free-trade economist, founder of the French Society for International Arbitration, and a friend and collaborator with Richard Cobden and John Bright. The famous peace activist explained that

> despite too many sad exceptions, the prevailing tendency is the rule of harmony and of universal agreement, which is so well expressed by the sublime idea of the unity and of the fraternity of the human race. The spring of that movement is exchange. Without exchange, human beings and whole peoples are lost brothers and become enemies. Through exchange, they learn to understand and to love one another. Their interests reconcile them and that reconciliation enlightens them. Without exchange, each stays in his corner, estranged from the whole universe, fallen in some way from the bulk of creation. . . . The doctrine of prohibition and of restriction not only preaches isolation and desolation but it condemns mankind to enmity and hatred.[72]

Passy dedicated his work to promoting freedom of trade and institutions of international arbitration as instruments for promoting peace and avoiding war.

Just as with the critics of war and empire in Europe, the same was true of the critics of American imperial ambitions and projects. The Anti-Imperialist League in 1898 was formed by business leaders, writers, and academics to oppose US military adventurism. One of their members, Yale professor William Graham Sumner, in his famous 1898 essay "The Conquest of the United States by Spain," argued that although the United States had beaten the Spanish Empire militarily and taken Guam, Puerto Rico, and the Philippines from Spain, it was in reality the principles of the Spanish Empire that had conquered the United States.

As Sumner concluded his stirring denunciation of imperialism and war, "We have beaten Spain in a military conflict, but we are submitting to be conquered by her on the field of ideas and policies. Expansionism and imperialism are nothing but the old philosophies of national prosperity which have brought Spain to where she now is. Those philosophies appeal to national vanity and national cupidity. They are seductive, especially upon the first view and the most superficial judgment, and therefore it cannot be denied that they are very strong for popular effect. They are delusions, and they will lead us to ruin unless we are hard-headed enough to resist them."[73]

What About "War for Oil (and Other Resources)"?

Actual colonial occupation is far less common today (although there are still examples), but it is not unusual to hear from people in many countries that overturning foreign governments, using military force and the threat or the initiation of war, and other exercises of government power beyond national borders, are necessary to secure resources. It's a reversion to the classical mercantilist logic refuted time and again by economists. Policy makers sometimes argue that war must be waged for economic reasons. In the present era, they argue that blood and treasure should be spent to secure access to oil. In 1990, then US Secretary of State James Baker testified before the United States Congress on behalf of undertaking the Persian Gulf War against Saddam Hussein's regime. He pointed to "the effects on our economy" and stated that

> this is not about increases in the price of a gallon of gas at the local service station. It is not just a narrow question of the flow of oil from Kuwait and Iraq. It is rather about a dictator who, acting alone and unchallenged, could strangle the global

economic order, determining by fiat whether we all enter a recession or even the darkness of a depression.[74]

One of his predecessors, Henry Kissinger, had earlier written in the *Los Angeles Times* to warn that the dictator of Iraq, Saddam Hussein, had "the ability to cause a worldwide economic crisis."[75] The issue of access to oil was raised again in the second US-led invasion of Iraq. Among other failings, those who supported going to war for oil failed to understand basic economics.

William Niskanen, then chairman of the Cato Institute and formerly a member of President Reagan's Council of Economic Advisors and a distinguished academic economist, stated in a public debate with former CIA director James Woolsey,

> Both in 1991 and in 2001, oil is not worth a war. The oil serves the interests of whoever controls it only if they sell it to us and to other people in the world. And American national interests are independent of the question of who owns that oil, with the exception of the question of the wealth of that country. Now that would be the case whether it was soybeans, rather than oil, and it's independent of whether we import a lot of oil or we were oil exporters. The price of oil in Japan is the same as it is in Britain, where Japan imports all of its oil and Britain is largely self sufficient in oil. We have a world market for oil. . . . So oil is not worth a war. It wasn't in 1991 and it is not now.[76]

Niskanen was right. Oil is a commodity and it has a global price. Even psychotic dictators realize that it's of little or no value if they don't sell it. Indeed, avowed enemies of the United States, such as the late Venezuelan dictator Hugo Chavez, understood that and sold most of the production of the state-owned oil company to American buyers.

But let's say that the flow of oil or some other resource might be reduced. What then? Well, economics informs us of two important points.

1. Military force is also costly. Indeed, it is almost invariably far more costly than any reduction in well being due to supply

restrictions from foreign governments. Advocates of military intervention assume that those military forces are costless. They're not.[77]

2. People interacting in markets have already discovered mechanisms to deal with supply reductions, notably the price mechanism; prices provide incentives to allocate goods to their most highly valued uses among competing uses (when prices rise, we "economize" on the use of scarce resources); rising prices provide incentives not only to conserve the resource, but also to increase supply and to shift to substitutes (in the case of petroleum, substitutes include natural gas, hydropower, solar, and other forms of energy). Relying on markets is far, far less costly than resorting to military force.[78]

Of course, mercantilist thinking and failure to take into account the costs of military intervention are not unique to the US government. Similar policies bankrupted the Soviet Union (each new satellite state added to their empire and imposed staggering burdens on the imperial power) and the People's Republic of China has been for some years paying substantial premiums for access to oil and other commodities. The policy has been quite costly to the Chinese taxpayers, as the state pays more than the market price (not counting additional inducements to political decision makers in other countries) and then subsidizes the use of such resources to loss-making state-owned enterprises.[79]

The French government has worked for many decades to gain special concessions for French business firms in West Africa; those concessions come at the expense of African consumers and of French taxpayers. The French government has sought to benefit French-owned businesses through maintenance of the CFA franc (CFA originally stood for *Colonies françaises d'Afrique* from 1945 to 1958, then *Communauté française d'Afrique*, and then after the independence of the French colonies *Communauté Financière Africaine*), foreign aid (a burden to French taxpayers, as US foreign aid is to US taxpayers and Chinese foreign aid to Chinese taxpayers), and the stationing of French military forces and periodic military intervention. The net beneficiaries are not "the French," but favored interests who benefit at the expense of the rest of the French population. As then French president Nicolas Sarkozy slipped into a discussion (caught by journalists) with Togo's elected president Faure Gnassingbé (who had been elected with the support of France), "When you're a friend of France, you have to think of French companies." The message was unmistakable and offered a peek into the world of modern cronyism.[80]

Similarly, the Russian government under president Putin has sought to create favors for Russian businesses, both state-owned and privately owned, by means of an aggressive foreign policy, including invasions of neighboring countries and annexation of territory, and the creation of a "Eurasian Customs Union." The result has been harmful to Russian consumers and taxpayers, but beneficial to owners and managers of firms that are close to the Kremlin, notably the "siloviki" who provide the muscle and support to that country's increasingly authoritarian regime.[81]

Free exchange is a far better way to obtain access to resources than the exercise of state power in any form. Mercantilism, imperialism, and militarism benefit narrow special interests, but they are contrary to the public interest. They're losing propositions.

Economic Fallacies and International Relations

Frédéric Bastiat, one of the greatest champions of liberty and peace and one of the best exponents of the values of libertarianism, declared a key mission of libertarian political economy: to explain that trade is mutually beneficial, whereas war is mutually destructive.

> Our mission is to fight against this false and dangerous system of political economy which considers the prosperity of one people as incompatible with the prosperity of another, which equates commerce with conquest and productive work with exploitative domination. So long as such ideas continue to be accepted, the world will never know twenty-four hours of peace. Even more, peace would be an incoherent and absurd idea.[82]

The persistence of such thoroughly debunked theories as the "balance of trade"—the idea that "the commerce of a nation is advantageous, in proportion as its exports exceed its imports"[83]—has caused enormous harm to the world. Rejecting spurious doctrines is not a matter of political ideology, but of sound economics, regardless of what other views one has about the world. As the trade economist Paul Krugman argued,

> The conflict among nations that so many policy intellectuals imagine prevails is an illusion, but it is an illusion that can destroy the reality of mutual gains from trade.[84]

The simple ignorance of economic nationalists and their mercantilist proposals, of people who insist that poorer developing countries are a threat to developed countries, or vice versa, because one or the other will simultaneously attract net foreign investment *and* run trade surpluses,[85] is breathtaking. We can hope that such ignorance will retreat before sound economic analysis and that we will not wait much longer for the day predicted by Jean-Baptiste Say:

> The day will come, sooner or later, when people will wonder at the necessity of taking all this trouble to expose the folly of a system, so childish and absurd, and yet so often enforced at the point of the bayonet.[86]

When Goods Cannot Cross Borders, Armies Will

Freedom of trade and investment creates peace among nations. It doesn't make war between states impossible, but it does make it less likely, and that's a worthwhile achievement. Classical liberals have long connected peace and commerce. As the German classical liberal John Prince-Smith argued in 1860,

> The international interconnection of the interests resulting from freedom of trade is the most effective means for the prevention of wars. Had we advanced so far as to see a good customer in every foreigner, there would be much less inclination to shoot at him.[87]

We now understand better the strong positive connection, not only between peace and the freedom of trade, but even between peace and the volume of trade. The more trade flows across borders and the more cross-border investment there is, the lower the likelihood that there will be war.

In 1748 the French philosopher and political thinker Montesquieu pointed out in his influential book *The Spirit of the Laws* that

> the natural effect of commerce is to lead to peace. Two nations that trade with each other have become reciprocally dependent; if one has an interest in buying, the other has an interest in selling, and all unions are founded on mutual needs.[88]

As Solomon W. Polachek and Carlos Seiglie concluded after examining conflicts, "Trading nations cooperate more and fight less. A doubling of trade leads to a 20 percent diminution of belligerence."[89] Cross-border trade—and especially cross-border investment—interests people in the maintenance of peace. Those who have *more* ongoing trading relationships or investments across borders are *less* likely to support war against their customers and business partners. The more the people whose livelihoods depend on the maintenance of trade, the greater the support for peace, because there will be more voices raised against disrupting those valuable relationships. And the greater the volume of cross-border investments, the greater the support for peace, for the rather understandable reason that people don't like to see their own stuff being bombed and blown up.[90]

As is widely understood, the foolish and destructive policy of "trade protectionism" (i.e., raising barriers to trade to "protect" existing domestic producers) of the 1930s contributed substantially both to the Depression and to the world war that followed.[91] Indeed, that was predicted by the 1,028 American economists who signed a petition against the extreme trade restrictions on over twenty thousand imported goods that was passed by the American Congress in 1930. That blow to American consumers (and to American exporters) ignited a wave of protectionism worldwide, deepened and lengthened the Depression in Europe and the United States, led to a collapse in world trade, and helped to pave the way for war. The concluding words of the petition were: "A tariff war does not furnish good soil for the growth of world peace."[92] And so it turned out to be.

After the horrors of World War II, US President Harry Truman observed in 1947,

> At this particular time, the whole world is concentrating much of its thought and energy on attaining the objectives of peace and freedom. These objectives are bound up completely with a third objective—reestablishment of world trade. In fact the three—peace, freedom, and world trade—are inseparable. The grave lessons of the past have proved it.

In that speech, President Truman noted that "as each battle of the economic war of the thirties was fought, the inevitable tragic result became more and more apparent."[93]

An Ancient Insight
The understanding that peaceful behavior and trade are connected goes back a very long time. In Book IX of the *Odyssey* the Greek poet Homer depicts the Cyclopeans, who eat those who land on their island, as savages. They lack the institutions of civilization, notably deliberation, laws, and trade.

> They have no meeting place for council, no laws either,
> no, up on the mountain peaks they live in arching caverns—
> each a law to himself, ruling his wives and children,
> not a care in the world for any neighbor.
> . . .
> For the Cyclops have no ships with crimson prows,
> no shipwrights there to build them good trim craft
> that could sail them out to foreign ports of call
> as most men risk the seas to trade with other men.[94]

Debate, discussion, criticism, trade, travel, investment, and other elements of free societies do not make wars impossible, but they do make them far less likely. They limit and reduce savage violence. And there is much to be said for that.

Who Decides?

Libertarians have always understood that it is naïve and superficial to assume that the wars waged by ruling elites are somehow to the advantage of the populations ruled by the states waging war. The historian Parker T. Moon put the matter quite clearly in his book *Imperialism and World Politics*:

> Language often obscures truth. More than is ordinarily realized, our eyes are blinded to the facts of international relations by tricks of the tongue. When one uses the simple monosyllable "France" one thinks of France as a unit, an entity. When to avoid awkward repetition we use a personal pronoun in referring to a country—when for example we say "France sent *her* troops to conquer Tunis"—we impute not only unity but personality to the country. The very words conceal the facts and make international relations a glamorous drama in which personalized nations are the actors, and all too easily we forget the flesh-and-blood men and women who are the true actors. How different it would be if we had no such word as "France," and had to say instead—thirty-eight million men, women, and children of very diversified interests and beliefs, inhabiting 218,000 square miles of territory! Then we should more accurately describe the Tunis expedition in some such way as this: "A few of these thirty-eight million persons sent thirty thousand others to conquer Tunis." This way of putting the fact immediately suggests a question, or rather a series of questions. Who are the "few"? Why did they send the thirty thousand to Tunis? And why did these obey?
>
> Empire-building is done not by "nations" but by men. The problem before us is to discover the men, the active, interested minorities in each nation, who are directly interested in imperialism, and then to analyze the reasons why the majorities pay the expenses and fight the wars necessitated by imperialist expansion.[95]

It is at best an abbreviation of the complex activities behind a war to say that "Country X made war on or sent soldiers to invade

Country Y"; in fact some group of people in Country X made choices with serious consequences for others and the task of a serious social scientist is to understand how and why those choices were made and why others complied with them. War is a choice, at least on the part of an aggressor. The attempt to aggregate all of the people, all of the interests, and all of the opinions found in a country into one organic choice-making agent is not only an example of mystical nonsense, but worse, it conceals from us all of the important questions of political science. Yet that is the approach taken by too many commentators, analysts, and ideologues of war and conflict. They fail to understand the issues involved because they are collectivists not only in morality, but in social science methods, as well. They think that a country, which is made up of huge numbers of diverse individuals and their complex relationships (families, networks, political parties, enterprises, religious affiliations, and on and on and on) is an individual just like the individuals who comprise it.[96] That is sloppy thinking with serious consequences.

Choices are made; they don't just happen. We respond to incentives, but we also are motivated by ideas. Foolish ideas provide support to foolish policies that create perverse—even catastrophically dangerous—incentives.

If you want peace, you need to stand up for it. If the case is made for war, it should be challenged. There's no such thing as being "undecided" about war. It's a binary choice. If you're not for it, you have to be against it; there is no neutrality on the issue of war itself. The destruction caused by war, the loss of innocent life, and the waste it entails create a very, very high presumption against going to war. Moreover, if you want others to want peace, you should not only speak out for peace, but combat the fallacies about "clashes of civilizations," "economic conflict," "protectionism," and the zero-sum worldview and actively support the institutions that create incentives for peace, notably freedom of trade, travel, and investment, and democratic rights of freedom of speech and criticism of government policy.

The historian Parker T. Moon's challenge, to "analyze the reasons why the majorities pay the expenses and fight the wars," is our challenge, too. And when we understand the issues, we should stand up for what is right—for the philosophy, the political economy, the institutions, the policies, and the realization of a peaceful world of voluntary cooperation.

7

THE AMERICAN ENLIGHTENMENT'S WARINESS OF WAR

By Robert M. S. McDonald

How did people come to see war not as an occasion for glory, not as the first resort, but as the last? What are the origins of the principle of civilian control of the military? What role did the American Enlightenment play in that process and who were the key figures? Robert M.S. McDonald is associate professor of history at the United States Military Academy and an adjunct scholar of the Cato Institute. He has published widely in scholarly journals and books on the American founding period and is an authority on the life and thought of Thomas Jefferson.

War was once taken for granted. It was considered a normal and even a positive part of life. In fact, it was celebrated—not only in the distant past, but also quite recently. Winston Churchill, a celebrated British statesman famous for standing tall against National Socialist tyranny during the Second World War, earlier had bragged of taking part in "a lot of jolly little wars against barbarous peoples." As he noted, "We proceeded systematically, village by village, and we destroyed the houses, filled up the wells, blew down the towers, cut down the shady trees, burned the crops and broke the reservoirs in punitive devastation."[97]

When World War I broke out, joyous mobs cheered in the streets of Europe's capitals. War was celebrated for the sake of national glory. War has also been celebrated for its alleged economic benefits: the supposed "stimulus" it provides by diverting productive resources toward the making of weapons and other instruments of destruction. (If anyone believes that it's a thing of the past to embrace the fallacy that broken windows and shattered lives can boost an economy, consider that Paul Krugman of the *New York Times* fatuously wished for an alien invasion to "stimulate" the United States economy.[98])

Today, while most would recognize that engaging enemies in war may be necessary to defend one's country or one's rights against aggression, armed strife is certainly not considered desirable for its own sake. War is now widely understood to be the last resort—not the first—and a threat to life, liberty, and prosperity. This more modern attitude toward war is rooted in the Enlightenment, a period of profound rethinking of the relations among human beings that included a reevaluation of warfare, which came to be seen as a negative kind of human interaction that rarely served to ennoble, civilize, or benefit either those who did the fighting or the nations for which they fought. As Thomas Jefferson wrote in 1797, "I abhor war, and view it as the greatest scourge of mankind."[99]

As Jefferson's statement suggests, the Enlightenment's reevaluation of war was especially profound among the thinkers who promoted the American Revolution, fought for the independence of the British colonies in North America, and founded the American Republic. Benjamin Franklin's dictum that "there has never been or ever will be any such Thing as a good War or a bad Peace" held true when provocations were light and transient.[100] Even when they were not—and war seemed necessary—the American founders understood that war possessed the potential not only to advance liberty but also to place it in peril. Armed conflict might be necessary to secure freedom and independence, but its effects could be pernicious. As James Madison warned, "Of all the enemies to public liberty war is, perhaps, the most to be dreaded, because it comprises and develops the germ of every other." War, Madison cautioned, could serve as an instrument of special interests. It was "the parent of armies," the costly institutions that spawned "debts and taxes" and joined with them to constitute "the known instruments for bringing the many under the domination of the few." In times of conflict, moreover, "the discretionary power of the Executive is extended; its influence in dealing out offices, honors, and emoluments is multiplied; and all the means of seducing the minds, are added to those of subduing the force, of the people."[101] Since war could do so much to increase the power of government, it could also do much to decrease the liberty of individuals.

Yet the purpose of government, as stated in the Declaration of Independence, was to secure individual liberty. Famous are the "self-evident" "truths" that "all men are created equal . . . with certain unalienable Rights," including "Life, Liberty and the pursuit of Happiness." Less often quoted are the important words that follow:

> to secure these rights, Governments are instituted among Men, deriving their just powers from the consent of the governed, That whenever any Form of Government becomes destructive of these ends, it is the Right of the People to alter or to abolish it, and to institute new Government, laying its foundation on such principles and organizing its powers in such form, as to them shall seem most likely to effect their Safety and Happiness.

In other words, when the people find that their government is destructive of the rights to life, liberty, and the pursuit of happiness, they may overthrow it and institute a new one to secure their "Safety and Happiness."[102] (Thomas Jefferson and the Continental Congress made no mention of glory or even economic stimulus.) The central dilemma of the War for Independence was how to construct a military powerful enough to defeat (or at least outlast) the army and navy of Great Britain—at the time the world's greatest superpower—but not so powerful as to pose a threat to the liberty for which the Revolution was fought. It was a conundrum that produced a creative tension resulting in checks on the military and a balance between its capacity for decisive action and its accountability to civilian control.

Well aware of usurpations by the likes of Julius Caesar and Oliver Cromwell—and heeding warnings about humanity's innate lust for power from ancient writers such as Tacitus as well as modern ones such as John Trenchard and Thomas Gordon—members of the Continental Congress turned to George Washington, a delegate from Virginia, to lead the Continental Army. While many factors made him an attractive candidate for the post, not to be overlooked is the fact that, after gaining military experience during the French and Indian War, he had spent the bulk of his adult life not in uniform but as a civilian legislator in the House of Burgesses, colonial Virginia's representative assembly. The selection of Washington did much to establish in America a tradition of military deference to civilian political leaders, with whom he engaged in candid correspondence but whose authority he never questioned.[103]

Given the ways in which members of the Continental Congress second-guessed Washington's prosecution of the war, his acquiescence to civilian control seems especially laudable. From nearly the start, Washington seemed to understand that time was on the side of the new nation. The longer the conflict dragged on, the greater the damage the British would inflict on themselves by alienating the American population through the heavy-handed and sometimes brutal treatment of civilians. A longer war also was more likely to undermine the will of the British government. Yet John Adams, anxious to avoid protracted bloodshed, in 1777 enthused that "my Toast is a short and violent War." Others agreed. The criticism became especially sharp when troops led by Washington failed to stop the British occupation of Philadelphia—a loss made more embarrassing by the victory at Saratoga of forces led by the Continental Army's second-ranking officer, Major General Horatio Gates. But the passage of time fostered appreciation for Washington's prudence and restraint. So did his clear consultation with and deference toward civilian leaders in the Continental Congress.[104]

Not all Continental Army officers followed his example. In a 1782 letter, Colonel Lewis Nicola conveyed to Washington the view of many officers when he suggested that government under the Articles of Confederation was too weak to effectively support the army. Washington shared this sentiment, but rejected Nicola's argument that an acceptable remedy might be seating him on a throne as America's king. He replied that the letter triggered "painful feelings . . . that such ideas are circulating in the army." The idea that military power should be the foundation of government, rather than popular consent and serving the people by securing their rights, was anathema to Washington and other figures in the American Enlightenment.[105]

Hostility to the new republic's civilian leadership did reemerge the following year, when an anonymous letter circulated among officers encamped with the Continental Army near Newburgh, New York. Lamenting poor prospects for pay, provisions, and pensions, the letter called for threatening Congress if it didn't meet officers' demands. Washington, hearing of the situation, convened a meeting at which he made a dramatic entrance, delivered a few remarks, and then—as he unfolded a letter he intended to read aloud to the gathering—shocked the audience by putting on a pair of glasses, which at the time were viewed as a sign of weakness and old age. "Gentlemen," he said, "you will permit me to put on my spectacles, for I have grown not only grey but almost blind in the service of my country." The statement impressed upon the officers the degree to which Washington—a man who had been with the Continental Army since the beginning, who refused to accept pay from the Continental Congress and had bullet holes in his coat—exemplified the ideal of virtue. To whatever extent the "Newburgh Conspiracy" posed a threat to civilian control over American government, the threat vanished at that moment.[106]

Frequently compared to Cincinnatus, the fifth century B.C. warrior-statesman who relinquished power after defeating Rome's enemies, Washington resigned his commission at the end of the war. He was happy to return to private life. In the months after his 1781 victory at Yorktown, he was eager to put the war behind him. "My first wish," he wrote, is "to see this plague to Mankind banished from the Earth; and the Sons and daughters of this World employed in more pleasing and innocent amusements than in preparing implements, and exercising them for the destruction of the human race." He hoped that, if war had to remain a European tradition, it would not take hold as an American one: "Rather than quarrel ab[ou]t territory, let the poor, the needy, and oppressed of the Earth; and those who want Land, resort to the fertile plains of our Western Country, to the second Land of promise, and there dwell in peace, fulfilling the first and great Commandment."[107]

Even in private life, former officers of the army continued to have a great deal of influence. They were prominent among the group of elected officials and other statesmen who, in 1787, supported replacing the Articles of Confederation with the Constitution. Among those advocates of a more centralized government was Washington, whose acquiescence to Madison's request that he preside over the Constitutional Convention lent legitimacy to the proceedings and reassured skeptical Americans that the new constitution would not be inimical to liberty. The Constitution granted to the central government significant new powers, especially in external affairs. Independent of the states, it could tax, raise, and maintain an army, declare war, and ratify treaties. Those powers were distributed among branches of the federal government. For example, while the new president (whom everyone seemed to know would be Washington) was commander-in-chief, the power to declare war was specifically delegated to the Congress. Although the president was empowered to negotiate treaties with other nations, it was the Senate that had the power to ratify or reject them and the House of Representatives that appropriated any funds needed to bring them into effect.[108]

Washington's presidency occasioned no wars but many foreign policy controversies. With Britain and France engaged in seemingly perpetual conflict, the commander-in-chief did his best to steer a neutral course. Pulled toward Britain by Federalists and toward France by Jeffersonian Republicans, Washington, at the end of his presidency, in his farewell address urged Americans to "cultivate peace and harmony" throughout the world and "observe good faith and justice towards all Nations." Washington insisted that "a free, enlightened, and, at no distant period, a great Nation" such as the United States should "give to mankind the magnanimous and too novel example of a people always guided by an exalted justice and benevolence." He asserted that "permanent, inveterate antipathies against particular Nations, and passionate attachments for others should be excluded; and that in place of them just and amicable feelings towards all should be cultivated." Why, he asked, would we ever make the foolish choice to "entangle our peace and prosperity in the toils of European ambition, rivalship, interest, humour or caprice?"[109]

Subsequent administrations struggled to live up to Washington's ideals. Jefferson, in his 1801 inaugural address, pledged "equal and exact justice to all men, of whatever state or persuasion, religious or political," and "peace, commerce, and honest friendship with all nations, entangling alliances with none."[110] But the national government did not always appear to embrace neutrality, or even abide by the Constitution—especially in times of international strife. One of the issues that galvanized Jefferson's supporters in the election of 1800 was President John Adams's 1798 signing of the Sedition Act, a measure empowering the government to jail for up to two years anyone who "shall write, print, utter, or publish . . . false, scandalous, and malicious" criticism of the president, Congress, or the laws of the United States. Passed during the undeclared Quasi-War with France, proponents of the measure presented it as a way to strengthen America against foreign and domestic enemies. Adams may have even used it to mollify more hawkish Federalists who wished for an all-out war that he had resolved to avoid. Jefferson and other opponents of the Sedition Act cast it as a clear violation of the First Amendment, ratified only seven years earlier, which promised that "Congress shall make no law . . . abridging the freedom of speech, or of the press; or the right of the people peaceably to assemble, and to petition the Government for a redress of grievances."[111]

Once in office, Jefferson also proved himself capable of expanding or exceeding the powers granted to the government in the Constitution—although always in ways that rendered war less likely. His 1807–1809 embargo of all international trade—a scheme envisioned as an alternative to war and an exercise in the "peaceable coercion" of Great Britain and France, each of which challenged Americans' neutral trading rights during the Napoleonic Wars—represented a very broad interpretation of Congress's Article I, Section 8 power "to regulate Commerce with foreign Nations."

Jefferson even privately confessed that the 1803 Louisiana Purchase violated the Constitution, which gave the national government no specific power to add new territory to the United States. But the measure, which doubled America's size and preempted the presence on its western frontier of a strong European rival, struck him as a necessary means to reduce the possibility of war. He worried that possession of the territory (and especially New Orleans) by France would render it "our natural and habitual enemy" and compromise American neutrality by causing the United States to "marry ourselves to the British fleet and nation."[112]

Despite Jefferson's efforts to preserve peace, his successor, President Madison, found that circumstances made armed conflict difficult to resist. The War of 1812 against Great Britain led to nearly calamitous consequences for the United States, which endured not only invasion but also internal dissent escalating to calls for secession in New England. Yet Madison proved himself almost unique among wartime presidents in that, even in the face of these threats, he took no actions that permanently expanded government power or even temporarily compromised civil liberty.[113] As Madison understood, the government's most basic responsibility was to use force, if necessary, to defend Americans against threats to their liberty. Providing government with such power, however, might enable it to undermine the freedom it was constituted to protect.

The acute awareness of this conundrum displayed by Madison and other luminaries of the American Enlightenment makes sense of the Revolutionary generation's pronounced preference for peace over war, its insistence on divided constitutional powers and other restraints, as well as its appreciation for leaders who exercised self-control. By no means perfect or perfectly consistent in their wariness of war (Alexander Hamilton and Aaron Burr, for example, possessed fairly conventional attitudes regarding the use of force), as a whole the men who rose to prominence during the movement for American independence stand out for seeking to avoid international strife, taking war off its pedestal, and inverting an age-old arrangement by placing the military under the control of civilians. They envisioned their new nation as an "empire for liberty" with the capacity for territorial expansion through the consent of white settlers petitioning for inclusion in a voluntary union of free and equal states.[114] (Indigenous inhabitants, whose property rights political leaders frequently overlooked, were seldom consulted.) Like Adam Smith, David Hume, Montesquieu, and the French thinkers known as "physiocrats,"[115] they dreamed less of conquest than of free exchange, which they believed possessed the potential to advance not only prosperity but also human knowledge, civilization, and brotherhood. Thomas Paine in *Common Sense* wrote that "our plan is commerce," which, "well attended to, will secure us the peace and friendship of all Europe." Subsequent events would temper Paine's idealism, but for the generation that took up arms and endured great hardships to secure independence, only the prospect of lost liberty could temper its aversion to war. "The strongest army our governments can ever have," Jefferson wrote in 1786, is "the good sense of the people."[116]

The achievements of the figures of the American Enlightenment were significant. They subjected military power to civilian authority. They erected intellectual, moral, legal, and political obstacles to war. Their achievements were partial and imperfect, in this area as in many others, as every student of American history well knows. They did raise a standard, however, of principles that changed the world, from the idea that "all men are created equal" to freedoms of speech and the press and the practice of placing civilians in charge of their military—upending the traditional practice in which the military controlled civilians. Although deep legal inequalities among persons persist, as do censorship and even military governments, the American Enlightenment provided moral and political standards that have endured. The safeguards against the folly of war by the Revolutionary generation were, as its members feared, eroded in the republic they established. Much of the later history of the United States demonstrates the power of war to concentrate power in the executive branch at the expense of the legislative branch, to increase secrecy in decision-making, to restrict civil liberties, and to increase debt and taxes. But those safeguards, weakened as they are, still exist and still continue to provide hope that liberty, limited government, and peace may be renewed, reclaimed, and extended.

8

WAR'S DECLINING SIGNIFICANCE AS A POLICY TOOL IN THE CONTEMPORARY AGE

By Justin Logan

Do wars succeed in achieving their stated objectives? What is the changing face of war in the modern world? What are the respective roles of material interests and ideologies in driving wars? Justin Logan is director of foreign policy studies at the Cato Institute. He writes in journals of foreign affairs such as *Foreign Policy*, the *Foreign Service Journal*, *Orbis*, and the *Harvard International Review* and regularly appears on broadcast media to discuss and explain international relations.

> *"[I]f you look back to the Korean War, there are very few instances where we have been militarily engaged in a major conflict where we have come out with what we saw as a victory, as clear cut as in World War II or in the first Gulf War in 1991."* —Robert Gates[117]

The modern world was shaped by war. Nation-states, the global economy, and the structure of the international system all owe part of their heritage to war.[118] As important a factor as war has been, it has also been in precipitous decline for centuries, as highlighted by Steven Pinker, James Payne, John Mueller, and other scholars.

Less well-appreciated is the fact that in wars in the modern era, initiators of conflict have rarely achieved their stated objectives. This essay discusses the types of wars fought during the period ending in 1945 and suggests reasons for their decline. Next, it describes the wars of the post-World War II period and explains why the initiators of those wars have rarely succeeded in achieving their goals. It concludes with lessons for policymakers and citizens.

The Rise and Fall of Major Power Wars

For millennia, tribes, city-states, kingdoms, empires, and nation-states fought one another in pursuit of additional territory and the opportunity to obtain valuable resources and increase their relative power.[119] In Charles Tilly's famous aphorism, "War made the state and the state made war."[120]

From the beginning of the modern era at the turn of the sixteenth century the frequency and lethality of war waxed and waned as states developed new organizations and technologies for violence, along with organizations and technologies for countering violence.[121]

Major powers fought wars of conquest with other major powers in efforts to seize resources, including mines, grazing lands, slaves, ports, gold and silver, and taxable subjects, as well as to convert populations to the religions or identities favored by the rulers.

Such wars have declined precipitously since the middle of the twentieth century. Some scholars have suggested that war has become less common because mankind as a species grew to think of war as a grotesque and uncivilized activity to a point where no one even thinks about the desirability of war anymore. It has become, in the words of John Mueller, "subrationally unthinkable."[122]

Norms evolve over time, but they are rarely completely independent of other, material factors. Changes in material developments spurred, or at least supported, that change in mindset. The sorts of wars great powers fought in the past are no longer so appealing, even to the most risk-prone leaders. Military technologies such as nuclear weaponry have made conquest a suicidal proposition in most cases. Non-military developments, such as nationalism and other forms of identity politics, have made conquered populations harder to control and assimilate. Economic developments, such as the horizontal integration of supply chains and the increase in cross-border trade, have made the prospective economic gains from war much lower.[123]

Among minor powers, of course, attempts at conquest have not ceased entirely. For example, Iraq invaded Kuwait in 1990 to gain control of the Kuwaiti oil fields and to void the financial debt the Iraqi state owed to the Kuwaitis. But the ease with which the US-led coalition dislodged Saddam Hussein's forces from Kuwait made clear that cross-border aggression is a risky proposition.

Contemporary Wars

While wars between major powers have declined dramatically, wars are still started. Three types of war persist, but they frequently fail to achieve their objectives.

Counterproliferation / Preventive War

Major powers, particularly the United States, regularly express grave concern about the acquisition of nuclear weapons technology and capability by other states. The 2003 Iraq War was justified primarily on the grounds of counterproliferation, despite the fact that the administration did not seek out and to some extent disregarded evidence that Iraq had no nuclear weapons program at all.

Though the doctrine of nuclear deterrence is widely accepted among major powers, those major powers oppose proliferation for a number of reasons. They fear the prospect of unintended nuclear war; they fear "proliferation cascades" or a nuclear "domino effect"; they fear the prospect of nuclear terrorism; and finally, they prefer to retain freedom of action against third parties. As Kenneth Waltz notes, "a big reason for America's resistance to the spread of nuclear weapons is that if weak countries have some they will cramp our style."[124]

Wars to counter the proliferation of nuclear weaponry, however, face a number of problems, the first of which was amply demonstrated in Iraq. The sort of intelligence needed for a successful counterproliferation war is difficult to obtain and frequently unreliable. Iraq provides an extreme case; Baghdad did not have a nuclear weapons program at all in 2003. Even in cases where nuclear programs are reliably known to exist, the comprehensive knowledge that would be required to hit enough key nodes of a developed nuclear infrastructure is terribly difficult to obtain.[125] The alternative would be regular strikes to set back efforts to rebuild the program, bombing the country every few years until it either relented in its pursuit of nuclear technology or there was "regime change" satisfactory to the attacker. Not only does it become difficult to think of a successful counterproliferation war, but threatening war to counter proliferation can even convince hostile states of the need for nuclear weapons to deter the potential attacker.

Counter-Domino / Wars for Influence and Credibility

Another goal of wars undertaken in recent decades has been the struggle for "influence" over weaker states by major powers. Major powers have frequently initiated or continued wars out of fear that a particular state may fall under the influence of another state, to the detriment of the intervener's security. The "domino theory" posits that either changes in the domestic politics of a given state or that state's coming into the sphere of influence of another state could cause a domino effect, with one domino knocking down the next and sending an unspecified number of other states into a rival state's embrace.

At this writing, Russian forces have invaded Ukraine. The Russian government claims the military units are not Russian, but rather Ukrainian self-defense forces, and that those forces are fighting political instability in Ukraine. The claim the forces are not Russian is risible and has not been credited by anyone outside Moscow's influence. The claim that they are fighting political instability rather than for continued naval access to the Black Sea via Crimea similarly does not withstand scrutiny.

While the Russian incursion shows military power is still relevant in international politics, the purpose of this essay is not to argue military power is irrelevant. Russian forces illegally invaded Ukraine, but there has been no war, partly because of Kyiv's correct judgment that there was little hope of resistance producing a favorable political resolution, and partly because of pro-Moscow sympathies among many residents of Crimea. The sorts of massive wars leaders undertook in the seventeenth or twentieth centuries belong in a different category than Russia's 2014 Crimean expedition. Stronger states bully weaker states when they feel it is easy and the stakes are high enough.

Such wars sometimes have catastrophic consequences for the intervener. Although it was already weakened by decades of economic mismanagement and overextended militarily, the Soviet Union's intervention in Afghanistan helped to destroy the Soviet state. The logic for intervening in Afghanistan—not a country rich in resources—is elusive, but evidence indicates that Soviet leaders feared that Afghanistan would turn away from Moscow and toward the West, and that this development would have underspecified but terrible consequences for the USSR's strategic position. As the war turned from bad to worse, Soviet leaders also began to fear that "the 'loss' of Afghanistan would be an unacceptable setback and a blow to Soviet prestige."[126]

Such logical chains of inference regarding influence and credibility frequently dominate the thoughts of interveners but rarely work in the way they fear. As Daryl Press has documented, credibility is not transferable in the way leaders believe it is. Statesmen tend not to evaluate present crises based on past behavior of adversaries. Rather, they evaluate their adversaries' material interests and military power in particular cases.[127] Similarly, influence itself tends to be contingent and ephemeral. States have rarely stayed loyal to a patron out of something other than their own perceived interest.

Humanitarian Interventions

Finally, states have intervened purporting to act on behalf of vulnerable or threatened third parties. It is sometimes difficult to identify such cases of humanitarian intervention clearly, because in order to sustain domestic support for interventions that are strategically irrelevant, governments frequently have insisted that the interventions were not, in fact, altruistic, but rather self-interested.

Notwithstanding the ostensible national-security justifications for the war, the 2011 US-led campaign in Libya is one recent example. Although US government officials continue to insist that intervention in the civil war there stopped a slaughter of perhaps

100,000 Libyan civilians in Benghazi by the Libyan regime, and counterfactuals are nearly impossible to prove, the claim is not plausible. The conduct of regime forces in Misrata, where fighting took place immediately before the targeting of Benghazi, did not indicate a policy of indiscriminate killing. Moreover, Libyan dictator Muammar Qaddafi threatened rebels with menacing language, but stated to civilians in Benghazi in a public address:

> Whoever hands over his weapons, stays at home without any weapons, whatever he did previously, he will be pardoned, protected. We will pardon anyone in the streets . . . Anyone who throws away his weapon and stays at home peacefully will be pardoned no matter what he did in the past. He is protected.[128]

His goal was to stay in power, not simply to punish his subjects. The fact that Qaddafi was a brutal dictator incited liberal sentiment in the West. Thus, anyone pointing out that claims that he had threatened to slaughter civilians were untrue risked looking like an apologist for tyranny. In addition, Western governments insisted that the future of Arab liberalization—the "Arab Spring"—hinged on preventing Qaddafi from winning the civil war.[129] Western officials went so far as to deny that their motive was regime change, despite a military campaign that made that objective obvious.[130] In any event, the war ended as have so many humanitarian interventions: regime change followed by a faltering economy and unresolved political divisions that endure beyond the limits of the attention spans of Western publics and policy makers.[131]

Conclusion

If wars rarely achieve the goals of the war makers, why do they continue to be launched? There is no single answer to that question, but a number of factors contribute to war-making.

States built institutions and supported the development of entire industries whose sole purpose was to prepare for war or to produce the infrastructure and the implements of war. The most famous comment on that phenomenon is President Dwight D.

Eisenhower's warning in his farewell address about the "military-industrial complex." Eisenhower, who had previously been a five-star general, warned that while scientific progress and a large defense industry were essential to military power and national defense, there was a risk that "public policy could itself become the captive of a scientific-technological elite." In other words, the military-industrial complex could "capture" US defense policy, causing at least orientations, if not policies, that would benefit arms manufacturers and defense contractors but were not optimal from a national-interest perspective.[132]

In the United States, the luxury of a reserve currency, geographic isolation from most severe threats, and a massive, resilient economy have amplified those dangers. US policymakers can waste resources subsidizing the military-industrial complex without obvious disadvantages to safety or wealth. States living closer to the margin of security and well-being face more demanding tradeoffs, and tend to start fewer frivolous wars. Because of America's security and wealth, many of the costs of foolish foreign policies are widely dispersed, and lead to fewer negative consequences for the leaders who pursue them.[133]

Finally, ideology plays an important role in enabling states to militarize society and wage war.[134] The bloody clashes of the twentieth century were fueled by the ideologies of nationalism, communism, fascism, and national socialism. Most ideologies give privileged place to the decisions made by one's own political leaders. From the French "mission civilisatrice," to the English belief in "the white man's burden," to the present day's "American exceptionalism," citizens believe that the superiority of their country grants it a special license to remake the world to its liking. Political leaders may even use religious rhetoric in speaking of the nation and its mission, thus infusing the national interest with the authority of God.[135]

Both material interests and ideologies, then, help to perpetuate wars. Wars can be made less frequent if both of those factors—material interests of military-industrial complexes and political elites, and ideologies of war and conflict—are countered. Those are worthy challenges for the rising generations of peace activists.

9

THE MILITARIZATION OF POLICING

By Radley Balko

> What is driving the increasing militarization of civilian policing? Why are police SWAT teams increasingly being established and equipped with the weapons of war, including tanks? Is it just happening in the United States or worldwide? What impact does the militarization of policing have on the relationship between the police and the public? Radley Balko is a journalist who currently blogs about criminal justice, the drug war, and civil liberties for the *Washington Post*. He is an investigative reporter for the *Huffington Post* and has been an editor at *Reason* and a policy analyst at the Cato Institute. He is the author most recently of *Rise of the Warrior Cop: The Militarization of America's Police Forces*.

Something is happening to policing. Gone are the "peace officers" of yesteryear. More and more police departments are coming to resemble—and to act like—armies. It's a trend that's noticeable in many countries. And it's a threat to domestic peace, law, and order.

In the United States between the early 1980s and today, police forces have undergone some pretty dramatic and fundamental changes. On the one hand, there are more civilian review boards and more internal affairs departments; most criminologists agree that there are fewer rogue cops—fewer "bad apples"—today than there have been in the past. On the other hand, whether it's serving warrants, responding to protests, or responding to crises, police agencies have become increasingly willing to use more force, more often, for increasingly petty offenses. In other words, there are fewer cops who use force outside of what's allowed by official policy. But it's what's now allowed by official policy that's troubling.

Most notable among the new policies is the ascent of SWAT (Special Weapons and Tactics) teams, task forces, and other aggressive police units that reflect varying degrees of military influence. For example, though they were once limited to large cities and reserved for emergency situations such as hostage takings, active shooters, or escaped fugitives, SWAT teams today are used far more often than they were a generation ago; moreover, they're primarily used to serve warrants on people suspected of nonviolent, consensual drug crimes.

The numbers are staggering. In the early 1980s, there were about three thousand SWAT "call-outs" per year across the United States. By 2005, there were an estimated fifty thousand. In New York City alone, there were 1,447 drug raids in 1994. By 2002, eight years later, there were 5,117—a 350 percent increase. In 1984, about one-fourth of towns between twenty-five thousand and fifty thousand people had SWAT teams. By 2005, that percentage had risen to 80 percent.[136]

In the past, that sort of force was reserved for emergency scenarios where lives were at immediate risk. It was the last option. Today, the use of such force is in many jurisdictions the *first* option when serving search warrants. SWAT teams today are used to break up poker games and massage parlors, for immigration enforcement, and even to perform regulatory inspections, raid bars suspected of serving under-age drinkers, and arrest people for unlicensed hair cutting.

Where the aim of SWAT was once to use violence to defuse an already violent scenario, today SWAT teams are primarily used to *create* violence and volatile confrontation where there was none before. The collateral damage has included the deaths of dozens of innocent people and nonviolent offenders, as well as police officers themselves, and thousands of people terrorized by screaming cops armed with battering rams, assault weapons, and flash grenades.

Moreover, local law enforcement agencies are being equipped by the US federal government with military equipment in the forms of heavily armored vehicles equipped with gun ports, tactical armor, grenade launchers, MRAP (Mine Resistant Ambush Protected) vehicles, and much, much more.

Troubling as all of that is, the problem goes beyond SWAT teams. Too many police departments today are infused with a more general militaristic culture. Cops today are often told that they're soldiers fighting a war, be it a war on crime, on drugs, on terrorism, or whatever other gremlin politicians have recently chosen as the enemy. Cops today tend to be isolated from the communities they serve, both physically (by their patrol cars) and psychologically, by an *us and them* mentality that sees the public not as citizens whom police officers are sworn to serve and protect, but as a collection of potential threats.

Police agencies today are also notoriously secretive. Internal affairs investigations are usually shielded from the public, and the unions that bargain on behalf of cops have fought hard—and in most places successfully—to keep personnel records private. Police unions have also persuaded many states to pass "police officer bills of rights," which confer special rights and protections on cops accused of crimes that aren't granted to regular citizens.

The United States is not alone in that trend. Britain and Canada now regularly conduct drug raids with SWAT-style police squads. In the 2000s, US officials used diplomacy and incentives to convince the Mexican government to enlist the country's military to fight the drug war. The results have included tens of thousands of homicides, mass corruption, and gruesome public executions.

The trend toward brute force is apparent in other parts of the world as well. In Brazil, paramilitary police forces such as the notorious BOPE (Batalhão de Operações Policiais Especiais, Special Police Operations Battalion) have turned the slums in cities such as Rio de Janeiro into urban war zones. Russia's OMON (Отряд мобильный особого назначения, Special Purpose Mobile Unit) squads have committed scores of human rights abuses, including the slaughter of refugees and brutally violent crackdowns on protesters. In Ukraine, a litany of abuses was committed by the country's now disbanded Berkut (Беркут, Golden Eagle) paramilitary units.

Following the disastrous riots at the 1999 World Trade Organization meetings in Seattle (which later investigations showed to be caused as much by police actions as by the actions of protesters), the default response to mass protest in the developed world has been brute force. Police typically meet protesters decked out in full riot gear. They go in *expecting* confrontation—a state of mind that tends to be self-fulfilling. In fact, the more important the conference, the more influential the conferees, and the more consequential their decisions, the more likely it is that protesters will be kept as far away from the event as possible—meaning the less likely it is that they'll be heard. That of course is the very antithesis of the value of free expression that free countries purport to embrace.

Certainly there are outstanding cops, great police chiefs and sheriffs, and plenty of police agencies that have healthy relationships with the public. There are national governments and local and municipal governments that effectively balance the maintenance of order with civil liberties and freedom of speech. Nonetheless, the ongoing militarization of policing is increasingly introducing the behavior and the attitudes of combat into the midst of civil society. Through the greater frequency in much of the world of SWAT raids and stop-and-frisk searches and the response to political protest with military force, the relationship between police and the public is growing increasingly antagonistic.

It would be a gross exaggeration to say that the US, Canada, or Britain has become a police state. An essay such as this one couldn't be published in a police state. But it would also be a grave mistake to wait until one lives in a police state to speak out against it.

10

THE PHILOSOPHY OF PEACE OR THE PHILOSOPHY OF CONFLICT

By Tom G. Palmer

What role do conflict and violence play in political life? Are there still people who glorify conflict? Who are the major proponents of conflict on the "left" and the "right" today and how influential are they? What is the central status of conflict in the ideologies of the left and of the right, and why and how is it different from how libertarians see conflict?

Πόλεμος πάντων μὲν πατήρ ἐστι πάντων δὲ βασιλεύς, καὶ τοὺς μὲν θεοὺς ἔδειξε τοὺς δὲ ἀνθρώπους, τοὺς μὲν δούλους ἐποίησε τοὺς δὲ ἐλευθέρους.

"War is the father of all and king of all, and some he shows as gods, others as men; some he makes slaves, others free."

—Heraclitus of Ephesus[137]

War was once the norm. Not merely human societies, but all the world was at war, shaped by war, bathed in war. War was inevitable. It was considered good. Although it occasioned suffering, that suffering was the necessary ground of human progress and virtue. The French reactionary writer Joseph de Maistre excitedly declared that war is "the habitual state of mankind, which is to say that human blood must flow without interruption somewhere or other on the globe, and that for every nation peace is only a respite."[138] Killing was the stuff of life.

That strikes most people today as strange and abhorrent. Something, or rather, some things, changed. War has become repulsive in the eyes of most people alive today.

There's a reason for the revulsion most people feel at the praise of war. A different idea has become dominant and the institutions that realize that idea now characterize most (but not all) human life in most (but not all) places in the world. The world is more peaceful than it has ever been. That may sound like a controversial claim, but it's supported by abundant evidence, which Harvard professor Steven Pinker examines in great detail in his book *The Better Angels of Our Nature: A History of Violence and Humanity.*[139] It's not only military conflict between states that has been declining for a very long time, but violence by husbands against wives, parents against children, and street criminals against their victims, each of which may tick up or down from month to month or year to year, but all of which are generally trending downward and have been doing so for a rather long time.[140] Among the causes that Pinker offers for the long-term downward trend in violence are:

- establishment of governments that can work to monopolize (and thus to some extent control) violence;
- the growth of commerce, which makes other people more valuable alive than dead;
- the gradual replacement of "honor" cultures by "dignity" cultures (in which avenging honor is less important than maintaining one's self control and dignity);
- the humanitarian revolution of the Enlightenment, with its emphasis on the value of human life, both one's own and the lives of others, and the replacement of superstition by reason and evidence (both of which were good news for people accused of "witchcraft," to take one example);
- the emergence and growth of international organizations, both of civil societies and of governments, to promote diplomacy

and mediation, rather than war;

- the invention and popularity of the novel, which was fueled by the free-market commercial revolution and which helped ever greater numbers of people to imagine that they were living the lives of others (and thus helped them to empathize with them);
- the increasing role of international exchange, investment, and travel in creating interests in the maintenance of peace;
- the greater acceptance of "the agenda of classical liberalism: a freedom of individuals from tribal and authoritarian force, and a tolerance of personal choices as long as they do not infringe on the autonomy and well-being of others";[141]
- the increasing importance, again fueled by the growth of commerce and technology, of abstract reasoning, which helps people to embrace general principles that are supportive of classical liberal/libertarian ideas of universal rights.

The story is a complicated one, because human history is complex, multi-causal, and varied. But it is an increasingly well-documented story and it refutes the claims of those who believe "that human blood must flow without interruption somewhere or other on the globe." Lasting peace is possible and not merely a "respite."

Toleration and coexistence, contract and cooperation, property and exchange have to a very great degree (but by no means entirely) replaced persecution and extermination, compulsion and struggle, theft and slavery, war and conflict as moral ideals. The movement that has changed the world and replaced war with peace, intolerance with toleration, looting with exchange has been known by different names at different times, but the most common is "liberalism," which in English-speaking countries is now called "classical liberalism" or "libertarianism."[142] Libertarianism is a philosophy that embraces peace. Peace is at the very core of libertarian thought, for it is at the core of the idea of liberty. "*Liberty* is to be free from restraint and violence from others," as the influential philosopher John Locke declared.[143] War is violence—directed, managed, applied, rationalized, glorified, furious violence.

Libertarians uphold peaceful and voluntary cooperation as both an ideal and a realistic possibility for human society. Other philosophies—those of the "left" and the "right," socialism, nationalism, conservatism, progressivism, fascism, communism, theocracy, and all the possible hybrids and permutations among them—posit instead that human life is inevitably a realm of strife, of conflict, of struggle, even of war, whether between classes or races or civilizations or nations or interests or religions.

The world has become more peaceful as libertarian values, principles, institutions, and practices increasingly permeate our lives. And an even more peaceful world will require that those values, principles, institutions, and practices be maintained, defended, advanced, and extended.

The Philosophy of Cooperation

Although many people and events contributed to the growth of libertarian ideas, the first systematic formulation of such ideas, combining toleration, freedom of trade, constitutional government, the rule of law, and equal rights, was by the English political movement of the seventeenth century known to history as the Levellers.[144] As Richard Overton announced from his prison cell in 1646, all property depends on property in one's own person, a right equally valid for every human being:

> Mine and thine cannot be, except this be. No man has power over my rights and liberties, and I over no man's.[145]

Overton and his colleagues articulated a radical vision of equal rights and of social harmony based on toleration of peaceful thought and action. To the idea of equal individual rights, based on moral philosophy, were joined the ideas of spontaneous order, namely, that social order can emerge without being deliberately designed and imposed by rulers, and of the rule of law, namely, that simple rules that are general, widely known, and equally applied create the framework for both the enjoyment of individual rights and the emergence of social order and harmony. That conception of a human order without violence, a society that would turn its back on war and conquest, horrified many, not merely aristocrats and soldiers, but some of Europe's greatest intellectuals, who raised fierce opposition to liberal ideas and practices. To many such thinkers, commerce was infinitely inferior to combat, liberty was merely a name for license, and toleration a rejection of God's laws.

Liberty, property, and commerce did have their defenders, who became bolder over time. The French thinker Montesquieu famously identified commerce with "gentle mores," that is, with gentle manners and behavior.

> Commerce cures destructive prejudices, and it is an almost general rule that everywhere there are gentle mores, there is commerce and that everywhere there is commerce, there are gentle mores.[146]

The role of commerce in creating gentle mores was implicitly acknowledged in the Greek language, for, as scholars have pointed out, the verb *katallassein* means "to exchange," but also "to admit into the community" and "to change from enemy into friend."[147]

A world of commerce, rather than glory, means a world of mutual gain, of positive-sum games, whereas glory entails conquest, and conquest entails defeat. Glory of that sort required antagonism. And it was that perceived loss of glory, and thus of virtue, that motivated so many to react against liberal ideas.

Just before his death, the libertarian economist and peace activist Frédéric Bastiat published an address "To the Youth of France," in which he laid out the key to understanding socialism. Socialists, he believed,

> felt that men's interests are fundamentally antagonistic, for otherwise they would not have had recourse to coercion.
>
> Therefore, they have found fundamental antagonisms everywhere:
>
> Between the property owner and the worker.
> Between capital and labor.
> Between the common people and the bourgeoisie.
> Between agriculture and industry.

Between the farmer and the city-dweller.
Between the native-born and the foreigner.
Between the producer and the consumer.
Between civilization and the social order.
And to sum it all up in a single phrase:
Between personal liberty and a harmonious social order.

And this explains how it happens that, although they have a kind of sentimental love of humanity in their hearts, hate flows from their lips. Each of them reserves all his love for the society that he has dreamed up; but the natural society in which it is our lot to live cannot be destroyed soon enough to suit them, so that from its ruins may rise the New Jerusalem.[148]

Bastiat anticipated the efforts of the collectivists of the twentieth century who, upon seizing control of states and thereby massive populations, set about trying to mold out of their fellow human beings the "New Man" who would embody their visions. Creating the New Man was the obsession of anti-liberal ideologues of both left and right, who merely differed on the details of what the New Man would be like. In contrast, "the economists," wrote Bastiat, "observe man, the laws of his nature and the social relations that derive from those laws. The socialists conjure up a society out of their imagination and then conceive of a human heart to fit this society."[149]

Human beings obviously do come into conflict. The classical liberal movement, in all its manifestations, was about seeking ways to deal with the problem of conflict. Religious toleration, limited government (which removes contentious issues from the scope of "public choice"), mediation and compensation in place of punishment, freedom of speech, and freedom of exchange were among the means classical liberals advanced to do so. The point was to reduce conflict and replace it with cooperation, rather than to celebrate it.

The Philosophy of Conflict

"I learned from this very four years' schooling in force and in all the fantastic extravagance of material warfare that life has no

*depth of meaning except when it is pledged for an ideal, and
that there are ideals in comparison with which the life of an
individual and even of a people has no weight. And though the
aim for which I fought as an individual, as an atom in the whole
body of the army, was not to be achieved, though material force
cast us, apparently, to the earth, yet we learned once and for all
to stand for a cause and if necessary to fall as befitted men. . . . It
is not every generation that is so favoured."* —Ernst Jünger[150]

Whereas classical liberals taught that human interests may be
reconciled peacefully through commerce, reason, democratic deliberation, and tolerance of peaceful differences, and that the right
institutions could lessen conflict and violence, their adversaries and
critics who were nostalgic for the old order began to formulate
theories based on the idea that conflict is an ineradicable feature
of human life, indeed, the one that gives it meaning. One of the
most influential enemies of the new philosophy of liberty was the
French reactionary Joseph de Maistre. He lashed out against the
idea of peace and praised war as the source of the best of humanity:
"The real *fruits* of human nature—the arts, sciences, great enterprises,
lofty conceptions, manly virtues—are due especially to the state
of war. . . . In a word, we can say that blood is the manure of the
plant we call *genius*."[151] Echoing Heraclitus, he insisted that "there is
nothing but violence in the universe."[152] That was the fundamental
view of the Counter-Enlightenment and of the thinkers who rose
up to attack the new ideas of classical liberalism.

The thinkers of the Counter-Enlightenment rejected the universal and embraced the particular; they rejected objective truths and
exalted creativity—not the creativity of the free individual, but of
the collective, into which the individual was submerged.[153] Markets,
merchants, and Jews, who were disproportionately represented
among European merchants, were reviled. Nations, classes, and
races could only seek their unique unity by clashing with other
nations, classes, or races. Steven Pinker observes that, in addition
to rejecting universality, objectivity, and rationality, "The Counter-
Enlightenment also rejected the assumption that violence was a
problem to be solved. Struggle and bloodshed are inherent in the

natural order, and cannot be eliminated without draining life of its vitality and subverting the destiny of mankind."[154]

That vision of relentless conflict pulsating at the core of human life, as well as the nostalgia for an imagined old order of settled relations, was taken up by socialist thinkers, notably Friedrich Engels and Karl Marx, who dismissed the liberal ideas of peace and trade, toleration and freedom as simple ruses that merely covered up and obscured from view another, deeper and more insidious, kind of conflict, violence, and exploitation. They acknowledged that liberal values acted to replace war with peace, theft with exchange, burning at the stake with toleration, national enmity with cosmopolitan toleration, but all that was waved away as occluding our view of deeper forms of violence. As Engels thundered in a pamphlet published in 1844,

> You have brought about the fraternization of the peoples—but the fraternity is the fraternity of thieves. You have reduced the number of wars—to earn all the bigger profits in peace, to intensify to the utmost the enmity between individuals, the ignominious war of competition! When have you done anything "out of pure humanity," from consciousness of the futility of the opposition between the general and the individual interest? When have you been moral without being interested, without harboring at the back of your mind immoral, egoistical motives?
>
> By dissolving nationalities, the liberal economic system had done its best to universalize enmity, to transform mankind into a horde of ravenous beasts (for what else are competitors?) who devour one another just because each has identical interests with all the others.[155]

Liberalism and free trade may have "reduced the number of wars," but only "to earn all the bigger profits in peace." The point deserves emphasis: Engels found bigger profits, which he abhorred (unless they were his), of far greater concern than reducing the number of wars.

The influential Victorian art critic and anti-Enlightenment Tory socialist John Ruskin waxed rhapsodic about the virtues of war and insisted that "no great art ever yet arose on earth, but among a nation of soldiers. There is no art among a shepherd people, if it remains at peace. There is no art among an agricultural people, if it remains at peace. Commerce is barely consistent with fine art; but cannot produce it. Manufacture not only is unable to produce it, but invariably destroys whatever seeds of it exist. There is no great art possible to a nation but that which is based on battle."[156]

For Enlightenment thinkers, in contrast—Voltaire, to take one prominent example—peace and social harmony were values in their own right, and not merely ruses to cover greater depths of social antagonism, as they were for Engels and Marx. Voltaire represented the values and perspectives of the Enlightenment when he praised exchange and toleration precisely because they produce peace.[157] The thinkers of the Counter-Enlightenment, such as Marx, de Maistre, and Ruskin condemned both exchange and toleration as degradations of human values.

Karl Marx and his co-author, collaborator, and financier, Friedrich Engels, identified liberalism with the newly emerged "class" they called the "bourgeoisie" (a term used rather promiscuously and inconsistently in their writings), which they accused of upending the whole order of the world and substituting cold calculation for warm social embrace. As market relations spread and intensified, barter (eggs for butter, for example) was increasingly being replaced by exchange mediated by money (eggs for money and then money for butter). That meant an increase in rationality generally, as people were able to compare alternate uses of scarce resources in terms of a common unit: money. That in turn facilitated rational accounting, including the precise calculation of profits and losses, which meant that more economic coordination was possible, more wealth could be created, the benefits of prosperity could be extended to ever-wider circles of people, and the interests and desires of ever more distant people could be taken into consideration. Marx and Engels dismissed such market-mediated rationality as "pitiless" and "the icy water of egotistical calculation." In *The Communist Manifesto* they asserted that liberal values, institutions, and practices merely *appeared* to be more humane, while in fact they replaced one form of violence with another, even worse, form.

The bourgeoisie, wherever it has got the upper hand, has put an end to all feudal, patriarchal, idyllic relations. It has pitilessly torn asunder the motley feudal ties that bound man to his "natural superiors," and has left remaining no other nexus between man and man than naked self-interest, than callous "cash payment." It has drowned the most heavenly ecstasies of religious fervour, of chivalrous enthusiasm, of Philistine sentimentalism, in the icy water of egotistical calculation. It has resolved personal worth into exchange value, and in place of numberless indefeasible chartered freedoms, it has set up that single, unconscionable freedom—Free trade. In one word, for exploitation, veiled by religious and political illusions, it has substituted naked, shameless, direct, brutal exploitation.[158]

The ideological leaders of the Counter-Enlightenment mounted a furious assault on liberalism and sought to realize various fantasies of collectivism in the new insular fraternities of nation, state, class, and race. In all cases, the message was that such groups of humans faced each other with essentially and irreducibly opposed interests. Solidarity, they believed, could be created only as the complement of enmity and hatred. As the insightful classical liberal novelist Robert Musil noted, "There is no getting away from the fact that man's deepest social instinct is his most anti-social instinct."[159] That vision has persisted among intellectuals who reject the values of reasoned deliberation, rational calculation through market exchange, toleration, and peace. Some of them may think of themselves as advocates of peace (openly extolling the benefits of military conflict is widely considered in poor taste in most contemporary intellectual circles), but they all embrace the core principle of essentially and irreducibly opposed interests, of struggle, of antagonism, of irreconcilable conflict. In their famous booklet of 1848, the two then-obscure intellectuals articulated a vision that inspired a movement that was to drench much of the world in blood.

> The history of all hitherto existing society is the history of class struggles. . . . Society as a whole is more and more splitting

up into two great hostile camps, into two great classes directly facing each other: bourgeoisie and proletariat.[160]

Marxists pursue class warfare and believe in the irreconcilable conflict between economically defined classes of people, one of which, the bourgeoisie, have to be "made impossible."[161] Fascists exult in war and violence as the purifying force that builds the nation.[162] National Socialists ("Nazis") seek the subjugation of "impure" or "inferior" races by the "Aryans" and laid down a challenge: "Those who want to live, let them fight, and those who do not want to fight in this world of eternal struggle do not deserve to live."[163] Critical theorists (influenced by Marx, with big helpings of Nietzsche, Freud, and whoever else was at hand to bash liberal toleration) believe that "bourgeois liberalism and tolerance are more often than not myths masking a 'will to rule.'"[164] Such anti-Enlightenment figures attack freedom of speech as merely a form of "repressive tolerance."[165] An army of illiberal academics have posited an array of "social forces" of domination—including class, gender, race, and other categories—that are more active and real than the mere flesh-and-blood "individuals" that surround us (although it takes the hard work of tenured professors to see those social forces properly and without distortion).[166]

Militarists extol war for alleged economic and moral benefits.[167] Neo-conservatives uphold the martial virtues as a noble ideal and an opportunity to "restore a sense of the heroic" to national life.[168] (The neo-conservatives hold "national greatness" to be a goal far greater, nobler, and more worthy than something so tawdry, debased, and un-American as "the pursuit of happiness.") "Realists" posit eternal enmity, or at best coldness, among states or even more broadly, "civilizations."[169]

Theocrats seek to subjugate all to God (or gods) through violence, with all professing one faith, one religion, one form of life, or, if that is not possible, at least a religious state that will subordinate and humiliate those of other religions, while generally expelling or killing those who profess no religion.

Many contemporary critics of classical liberalism, including the "Analytical Marxists," posit that there is no more violence in socialism than in any system, for all systems of decision making over scarce resources justify the use of force, if only to repel the use of force.[170] That is an old criticism of liberalism, dating back to at least the seventeenth century, when Sir Robert Filmer penned his defense of the divine right of absolute monarchy and argued,

> A great deal of talk there is in the world of the freedom and liberty that they say is to be found in popular commonweals. It is worth the inquiry how far and in what sense this speech of liberty is true: "true liberty is for every man to do what he list, or to live as he please, and not to be tied to any laws." But such liberty is not to be found in any commonweal, for there are more laws in popular estates than anywhere else, and so consequently less liberty; and government, many say, was invented to take away liberty, and not to give it to every man. Such liberty cannot be; if it should, there would be no government at all.[171]

Thus, according to that mode of thinking, a regime of forbidding rape is no less coercive than a regime requiring rape, for repelling a rapist is no less forceful than is raping. There is, according to that view, a quantum of violence in the world, which neither increases nor decreases.[172] Libertarians firmly deny that and refuse to equate raping with repelling rape.

The Friend-Enemy Distinction

Of all the contributors to the Counter-Enlightenment's rejection of classical liberal views about peace and the resolution of conflict, the most influential of the past century was Carl Schmitt, a legal theorist whose book *The Concept of the Political* came to have an enormous influence on both the anti-liberal "right" and the anti-liberal "left." He was "the century's most brilliant enemy of liberalism."[173] Schmitt posited that "the specific political distinction . . . can be reduced to that between friend and enemy."[174]

Schmitt insisted that liberals were wrong about social harmony, wrong that exchange was a moral alternative to conquest, wrong that debate could replace combat, wrong that toleration could replace animosity, and wrong that a world without enemies was even possible. For Schmitt, conflict was definitive of the political as such, and the political was essential to the human being. His influence on the political thought of the last century has been subtle and, because of his disgraceful and reprehensible life, often unacknowledged, but his core idea came to permeate the thinking of both the left and the right and inspired both "left-wing" and "right-wing" attacks on toleration, on the market economy, on limited government, on free trade, and on peace. Schmitt's ideas are also driving a resurgence of Fascist thought in Europe, as, for example, in the work of Moscow State University lecturer Aleksandr Dugin, whose work is a thinly veiled restatement of National Socialist ideology, with an expansionist "Russia" in place of "Germany" and "Eurasia" in place of the "Third Reich."[175]

For Schmitt, "The enemy is not merely any competitor or just any partner of a conflict in general. He is also not the private adversary whom one hates. An enemy exists only when, at least potentially, one fighting collectivity of people confronts a similar collectivity."[176] Indeed, "only in real combat is revealed the most extreme consequence of the political grouping of friend and enemy. From this most extreme possibility human life derives its specifically political tension."[177]

The Marxist philosopher Slavoj Žižek recognized that both left and right flavors of anti-liberal political thought embrace Schmitt's friend–enemy distinction and, as a "leftist," Žižek distinguishes the right's focus on external enemies from the left's "unconditional primacy of the inherent antagonism as constitutive of the political":

It is deeply symptomatic that, instead of class *struggle*, the radical Right speaks of class (or sexual) *warfare*. The clearest indication of this Schmittian disavowal of the political is the primacy of external politics (relations between sovereign states) over internal politics (inner social antagonisms) on which he insists: is not the relationship to an external Other as the enemy a way of disavowing the *internal* struggle which traverses the social body? In contrast to Schmitt, a leftist position should insist on the unconditional primacy of the inherent antagonism as constitutive of the political.[178]

For such thinkers, whether of the left or the right, conflict—
"inherent antagonism"—is constitutive of human life together.
(Even such a contemporary center-left progressive thinker as John
Rawls incorporates into his theory of social justice an inherent
conflict between citizens, in the form of the distinction between
the justice of the acts of the citizens and the justice of the overall social order, for even when "everyone with reason believes
that they are acting fairly and scrupulously honoring the norms
governing agreements . . . the tendency is rather for background
justice to be eroded even when individuals act fairly; the overall
result of separate and independent transactions is away from and
not toward background justice."[179] That is, conflict between the
interests of social groups is embedded in the very structure of justice, for although by stipulation everyone acts in accordance with
their rights and with the rules of justice, the outcome is inherently
unjust and conflicted, and the state must intervene to impose a
new just ordering on society, entirely independent of the rules of
just conduct among persons.)

In the years following World War II a "Carl Schmitt industry"
of publications has emerged on the far left; the influential Marxist
Telos journal embraced Schmitt's theoretical foundation of politics
for their anti-liberal program[180] and his ideas play a central role in
the influential, bitter, and violent attack on liberalism and peace,
promoted as "the new Communist Manifesto," by Italian leftist
writer Antonio Negri (who served prison time for his involvement in violence, including murder in Italy) and the American
literary theorist Michael Hardt.[181] Their book, *Empire*, a virtually
unreadable screed published by Harvard University Press just
before the 9/11 attacks on the Twin Towers in New York, prefig-
ured those attacks with its call for attacks on "global capital," its
definition of "the enemy" as "a specific regime of global relations
that we call Empire,"[182] its chilling remarks about radical Islamist
fundamentalism as just another form of postmodernism, and its
calls for "the potential of the multitude to sabotage and destroy
with its own productive force the parasitical order of postmod-
ern command."[183] (Hardly a sentence in the book is clear and

understandable, undoubtedly because of the extreme violence and hatred of the authors' philosophy; as George Orwell explained, "When there is a gap between one's real and one's declared aims, one turns as it were instinctively to long words and exhausted idioms, like a cuttlefish squirting out ink."[184])

Negri and Hardt draw inspiration from Schmitt's notorious defense of the Third Reich's "Großraum" approach to geo-political relationships. Schmitt sought to advance "the task of German jurisprudence to escape from the false alternative of, on the one hand, the merely conservative maintenance of the interstate way of thinking that has prevailed until now and, on the other hand, a non-stately, non-national overreach into a universalistic global law as carried out by the Western democracies. It must find between these two the concept of a concrete great spatial order, one that corresponds to both the spatial dimensions of the earth as well as our new concepts of state and nation."[185] It is the "non-stately, non-national overreach into a universalistic global law as carried out by the Western democracies" that Negri and Hardt termed "Empire" and whose destruction through violence they promoted.

Schmitt's ideas and conceptions of politics are also entwined with far-right and neo-conservative thought, the latter largely through the influence of the philosopher Leo Strauss, who himself had a major influence on Schmitt,[186] and Strauss's influential American followers, such as former White House adviser William Kristol, editor of *The Weekly Standard* and an architect of the Iraq War,[187] and *New York Times* columnist David Brooks, who calls for "national greatness conservatism."[188] In its less militant form such conservatism amounts to a call for building huge state monuments to national greatness. In its more militant form, it calls openly for war; the neo-conservatives were a primary driving force behind the invasion of Iraq and continue to press for military confrontation at almost every turn. Waging war, according to William Kristol and Robert Kagan, would restore "a true conservatism of the heart," which "ought to emphasize both personal and national responsibility, relish the opportunity for national engagement, embrace the possibility of national greatness, and restore a sense of the heroic, which has been sorely lacking from American foreign policy—and from American conservatism—in recent years."[189]

Schmitt was deeply influenced by Leo Strauss's comments on his work and at Strauss's suggestion reformulated his ideas to make them even more thoroughly anti-liberal. Strauss had commented on the 1932 edition of *The Concept of the Political* and concluded that Schmitt had not rejected liberalism sufficiently and was still trapped within categories established by liberalism. Strauss concluded: "We said Schmitt undertakes the critique of liberalism in a liberal world; and we meant thereby that his critique of liberalism occurs in the horizon of liberalism; his unliberal tendency is restrained by the still unvanquished 'systematics of liberal thought.' The critique introduced by Schmitt against liberalism can therefore be completed only if one succeeds in gaining a horizon beyond liberalism."[190] And that Schmitt proceeded to do; in the 1933 edition, which was published after Hitler's victory but suppressed after the war (subsequent editions of the book were reprints of the 1932 edition), Schmitt endorsed National Socialism, made his anti-Semitism more explicit, and phrased the conflict between friend and enemy in clearly racial terms.[191] (There is a very disturbing irony in a Jewish intellectual's penetrating criticisms convincing and encouraging a German intellectual to become an avid Nazi and the "foremost Nazi jurist"[192] of the Third Reich.)

For Schmitt, as for Marx and Engels, free trade was not a peaceful alternative to war, but merely a cover for a more brutal form of exploitation. "The concept of humanity is an especially useful ideological instrument of imperialist expansion, and in its ethical-humanitarian form it is a specific vehicle of economic imperialism."[193] Liberal conceptions of universal human rights were rejected as incompatible with his distinction between friend and enemy:

> Humanity is not a political concept, and no political entity or society and no status corresponds to it. The eighteenth-century humanitarian concept of humanity was a polemical denial of the then existing aristocratic-feudal system and the

privileges accompanying it. Humanity according to natural law and liberal-individualistic doctrines is a universal, i.e., all-embracing, social ideal, a system of relations between individuals. This materializes only when the real possibility of war is precluded and every friend and enemy grouping becomes impossible. In this universal society there would no longer be nations in the form of political entities, no class struggles, and no enemy groupings.[194]

Not for him any appeals to liberal ideas such as universal human rights, or toleration, or freedom of speech, trade, and travel.

All liberal pathos turns against repression and lack of freedom. Every encroachment, every threat to individual freedom and private property and free competition is called repression and is *eo ipso* evil. What this liberalism still admits of state, government, and politics is confined to securing the conditions for liberty and eliminating infringements on freedom.

We thus arrive at an entire system of demilitarized and depoliticized concepts.[195]

A "demilitarized and depoliticized" world meant also, for Schmitt (and for Strauss, Jünger, and others of that tradition), a world of unseriousness, of mere "entertainment." A truly human world is a politicized world, and "the political is the most intense and extreme antagonism, and every concrete antagonism becomes that much more political the closer it approaches the most extreme point, that of the friend-enemy grouping."[196] Whether the enemy is external or internal, it is the focal point of life for both right and left. Titanic and heroic forces must be pitted against each other in a struggle worthier, higher, more noble than the life of "entertainment," of business, of trade, of family, of love, all of which are unserious compared to "the political." To live the serious political life, peaceful cooperation, toleration, and the plurality of lives lived "from the inside"—all the values of liberalism—must be suppressed and social forces must be focused on defeating *the enemy*.

The Ideas of 1914

> *"We stand in the memory of the dead who are holy to us, and we*
> *believe ourselves entrusted with the true and spiritual welfare*
> *of our people. We stand for what will be and for what has been.*
> *Though force without and barbarity within conglomerate in*
> *somber clouds, yet so long as the blade of a sword will strike a*
> *spark in the night may it be said: Germany lives and Germany*
> *shall never go under!"*   —Ernst Jünger[197]

The intellectual movement of which Schmitt was such an important figure included many others who were deeply influenced by "The Ideas of 1914," a celebration of the year that Europe plunged into mass hysteria and millions were killed.[198] The experience of the war had an enormous influence worldwide, not only in political matters (centralizing government power in the United States, for example), but in creating a cult of conflict, regimentation, and war. Ernst Jünger's brilliant work *The Storm of Steel* was an especially significant work in that tradition. (Jünger was also a close correspondent of Schmitt; they carried on an intense exchange of letters for over fifty years.[199])

Jünger, like his friend and correspondent Schmitt, was an intellectually powerful figure who influenced both right and left against libertarian values and ideas.[200] His account of his experiences as a storm trooper in World War I was a popular statement of "The Ideas of 1914," notably its militaristic collectivism. In *The Storm of Steel*, Jünger glorified struggle and conflict through war. The implicit contrast was the boredom, the sheer pointlessness, the lack of seriousness of life at peace, of making things and selling and buying them, of going to concerts and plays, laboratories and art galleries, of pursuing scientific knowledge, of enjoying a good beer with good friends. The bourgeois life was dull, whereas the life of struggle, of violent death, of war was the only condition under which one could truly live.

> And if it be objected that we belong to a time of crude force our answer is: We stood with our feet in mud and blood, yet

our faces were turned to things of exalted worth. And not one of that countless number who fell in our attacks fell for nothing. Each one fulfilled his own resolve.

. . .

When once it is no longer possible to understand how a man gives his life for his country—and the time will come—then all is over with that faith also, and the idea of the Fatherland is dead; and then, perhaps, we shall be envied, as we envy the saints their inward and irresistible strength.[201]

That was how Jünger and many others saw the war, but that was probably not how it was seen by millions of other soldiers who drowned in the sucking mud, whose lungs were burned by mustard gas and who died coughing out gobbets of blood, who never saw again their wives, their children, their sweethearts, their friends. Erich Maria Remarque, who wrote *All Quiet on the Western Front,* described the war quite differently. Jünger was celebrated, but Remarque's works were burned by the National Socialists and his sister was beheaded under orders of a National Socialist "judge" of the "Volksgerichtshof" ("People's Court") who was reported to have declared, "Your brother has escaped us, but you will not."[202]

Jünger was no mere artist, but through his aesthetic appreciation of violence, conflict, and regimentation an active promoter of totalitarian dictatorship. As he wrote on behalf of dictatorship,

The genuine revolution has certainly not yet happened. It marches inexorably onward. It is no reaction, but rather an actual revolution with all its characteristics and manifestations. Its idea is that of the Folk, honed to as yet unknown sharpness; its banner is the swastika; its outward expression the concentration of the will in a single point—dictatorship! The dictatorship will replace word with deed, ink with blood, the phrase with sacrifice, the pen with the sword.[203]

"Total Mobilization" as a concept was introduced by Jünger in his 1930 essay and excited Germany's anti-liberal collectivists (Martin Heidegger among them) as a vision of technologically enabled collectivism. He praised "the increasing curtailment of 'individual liberty,' a privilege that, to be sure, has always been questionable," marveled at how in the Soviet Union "for the first time, the Russian 'five-year plan' presented the world with an attempt to channel the collective energies of a great empire into a single current," and referred to "Total Mobilization" as "merely an intimation of that higher mobilization that the age is discharging upon us."[204]

The choice of dictatorship, of *anything but liberalism*, shows the deep affinity of the rival forms of collectivism. Jünger reminisced late in life about his early pro-Soviet attitudes (before working for the Third Reich); of the Soviet Union, he said,

> I was very interested in the plan, the idea of the plan. I told myself: granted, they have no constitution, but they do have a plan. This may be an excellent thing.[205]

It is worth contrasting the appreciation of collectivism by Jünger and his circles to the very different response of the Russian writer Vasily Grossman, who grew up under the regimentation of Soviet collectivism and came to reject it; he saw clearly the underlying sameness of fascism, national socialism, and communism. Grossman was a writer for *Red Star*, the Red Army newspaper, and the first person to write an account of the liberation of one of the Third Reich's death camps, Treblinka. Grossman, who had never lived in a free society, came to understand and to yearn for liberty. His novel *Life and Fate* was not published in his lifetime; it (along with the typewriter ribbon with which it was typed) was seized by the KGB upon completion. In *Life and Fate*, in the midst of the war between the Third Reich and the Soviet Union, Red Army Colonel Pyotr Pavlovich Novikov inspects the soldiers assembled under his command and realizes,

> Human groupings have one main purpose: to assert everyone's right to be different, to be special, to think, feel, and live in his or her own way. People join together in order to win or defend this right. But this is where a terrible, fateful error is

born: the belief that these groupings in the name of a race, a God, a party, or a State are the very purpose of life and not simply a means to an end. No! The only true and lasting meaning of the struggle for life lies in the individual, in his modest peculiarities and in his right to those peculiarities.[206]

Such "modest peculiarities" provide no inspiration to the collectivist ideologues of left and right, who are intent on enlisting and regimenting the rest of us in their greater causes and struggles.

Jünger's influence continues. One can hear his voice quite distinctly in the writings of *New York Times* neo-conservative writer David Brooks. In a column of August 23, 2010, titled "A Case of Mental Courage," Brooks quotes the novelist Fanny Burney's description of the gruesome experience of a mastectomy without anesthesia ("I then felt the Knife rackling against the breast bone—scraping it! This performed while I yet remained in utterly speechless torture.") and praises the very experience of it and her "heroism" in recounting it in every detail ("an arduous but necessary ordeal if she hoped to be a person of character and courage"). Brooks echoes Jünger's influential 1934 essay "On Pain," which dismissed the advances of the Enlightenment and stated "with some certainty that the world of the self-gratifying and self-critical individual is over and that its system of values, if no doubt still widespread, has been overthrown in all decisive points or refuted by its own consequences."[207]

According to Brooks, "Heroism exists not only on the battlefield or in public but also inside the head, in the ability to face unpleasant thoughts." Moreover, echoing Schmitt, Jünger, and Strauss, Brooks bemoans liberal capitalism: "There's less talk of sin and frailty these days. Capitalism has also undermined this ethos. In the media competition for eyeballs, everyone is rewarded for producing enjoyable and affirming content." Life has been reduced to merely "enjoyable and affirming" content and lacks the "heroic," themes that echo the complaints of Strauss and Schmitt that free societies lack seriousness. Brooks, also an eager champion of going to war in Iraq, in his writings offers an aesthetic expression of the call of his fellow neo-conservatives Robert Kagan and William

Kristol to "restore a sense of the heroic" to the United States by using its military power to "contain or destroy many of the world's monsters."[208]

That a nation may be great without war, without violence, without antagonism, through the protection of the rights of individuals to the peaceful enjoyment of their modest peculiarities is simply unthinkable for the inheritors of the tradition of collectivism. For them, life without heroic struggles is life without seriousness, life without meaning. That aesthetic valorization of war provided the fuel that consumed the lives of millions.

Wars Are Not Inevitable

"Soon there will be no poor so foolish as to go to war; not because it has become unprofitable, for it has never been profitable; but because social consciousness has been developed by the teachings of the great libertarians, who have always stood for peace. Liberty leads to peace, while authority leads to war. Lovers of liberty are willing to compare the lives of those who stood for liberty with those who have stood for authority, of those who have tried to save with those who have tried to destroy." —Charles T. Sprading[209]

In 1913, shortly before a fantastically deadly and destructive war broke out in Europe, an American libertarian pre-empted the coming rhetoric of Woodrow Wilson, the US president who took the United States into what he called a "war to end all wars." Charles T. Sprading asked,

How is war to be stopped? By going to war? Is bloodshed to be stopped by the shedding of blood? No; the way to stop war is to stop going to war.[210]

The voices of the libertarians of the day were not heeded and millions paid with their lives. The tide had turned against liberty, as the libertarian journalist E.L. Godkin had warned at the turn of the century:

Only a remnant, old men for the most part, still uphold the Liberal doctrine, and when they are gone, it will have no champions. . . . The old fallacy of divine right has once more asserted its ruinous power, and before it is again repudiated there must be international struggles on a terrific scale.[211]

Godkin was right about the short term and Sprading was wrong. But both of them saw a longer term that promised peace. The tide has turned again toward the ideas of liberty. Libertarians on every continent are working for a world of peace and freedom of thought, speech, worship, love, association, travel, work, and trade. The growth of a global economy has diminished the incentives for war and increased the chances for peace.

It is up to us to repudiate, once and for all, the modern theories of the "divine right" of rulers, statesmen, and warlords to dispose of the lives of others. It is time, in the words of Colonel Pyotr Pavlovich Novikov, "to assert everyone's right to be different, to be special, to think, feel, and live in his or her own way," and to realize a world in which all enjoy liberty and peace.

11

THE ART OF WAR

By Sarah Skwire

> How does literature and poetry allow us to see what
> is otherwise hidden from view in war? What advantage
> does the poet have compared to the statistician, the
> historian, and the journalist in helping us to understand
> war? Sarah Skwire is the author of the college writing
> textbook *Writing with a Thesis*, currently in its eleventh
> edition, and has won prizes for her poetry, which has
> appeared in *The New Criterion*, *The Oxford Magazine*, and
> the *Vocabula Review*, among other places. She is a fellow
> at the Liberty Fund.

Nearly lost amid the grand historical events and the epic characters
of Shakespeare's *Henry V* is the unnamed child known simply, in
the list of characters, as "Boy." He hangs out with Hal's former
companions as they prepare to serve in a war against France begun
by their old friend who is now the king. We scarcely notice the
boy's small part in the play until, towards the end of Act 4, he helps
the comic character Pistol by translating some French, and then
turns to tell the audience, "I must stay with the lackeys, with the
luggage of our camp: the French might have a good prey of us, if
he knew of it; for there is none to guard it but boys."

And that is the last that we hear from the boy, for the French
do know of it. The boys guarding the luggage are slaughtered,
and this "arrant piece of knavery" is one more bloody moment in
a play that is preoccupied with weighing the balance between the
glories and horrors of war.

But why would Shakespeare take the time to do this? Why pause in the middle of the Battle of Agincourt, for heaven's sake, to give an extra speech to a nameless child who is about to die?

The answer, I think, is that we need the story of the boy, and our horrified response to it, as a vaccine against Falstaff's callous attitude towards his soldiers in *I Henry IV*. "Tut, tut, good enough to toss; food for powder, food for powder. They'll fill a pit as well as better. Tush, man, mortal men, mortal men." The answer, I think, is that Shakespeare understood that one of the most powerful things literature can do—amid the totalizing, anonymizing experience of war—is to help us hear the voice of the individual. And it is that capability that makes literature so valuable for classical liberals who want to study and understand war in order to eliminate it.

That war anonymizes us is not a new assertion. Orwell knew it well, and in his novel *1984*, which portrays a world that has "always been at war," we see a whole new social order created to aid in that anonymizing. Men and women are discouraged from forming intimate relationships. All activities are group activities. There is constant surveillance, and a disallowing of any private space, or any personalized possessions, all intended to create interchangeable units out of individual humans.

When Vaclav Havel writes of a post-totalitarian state that has moved from violence into a grim and settled acceptance of its oppressive government he could just as easily be describing a state at war: "Between the aims of the post-totalitarian system and the aims of life there is a yawning abyss: while life, in its essence, moves toward plurality, diversity, independent self-constitution, and self-organization, in short, toward the fulfillment of its own freedom, the post-totalitarian system demands conformity, uniformity, and discipline.... This system serves people only to the extent necessary to ensure that people will serve it. Anything beyond this, that is to say, anything which leads people to overstep their predetermined roles is regarded by the system as an attack upon itself."

Against this anonymizing and destructive force of war and of the state at war, we have the voice of the writer.

Mark Twain uses this power in *The War Prayer* when his heavenly prophet reminds the assembled congregation that their prayer for victory is also a prayer for others' destruction:

> O Lord our God, help us tear their soldiers to bloody shreds with our shells; help us to cover their smiling fields with the pale forms of their patriot dead; help us to drown the thunder of the guns with the shrieks of their wounded, writhing in pain; help us to lay waste their humble homes with a hurricane of fire; help us to wring the hearts of their unoffending widows with unavailing grief; help us to turn them out roofless with their little children to wander unfriended . . . imploring thee for the refuge of the grave and denied it.

When the enemy is no longer an anonymous mass, it is much harder to shoot at them.

And when one is no longer part of an anonymous mass, it is harder to do the shooting. That is why regimentation is so important. Henry Reed's poem "Easing the Spring," written during WWII, presents us with a class on handling weaponry, where new recruits are being molded into soldiers. The droning voice of the drill sergeant and the regimentation he is teaching are contrasted with the beautiful spring day and the wildness of nature just outside the classroom.

> To-day we have naming of parts. Yesterday,
> We had daily cleaning. And to-morrow morning,
> We shall have what to do after firing. But to-day,
> To-day we have naming of parts. Japonica
> Glistens like coral in all of the neighboring gardens,
> And to-day we have naming of parts.

But of course, the anonymizing of war is sinister not merely because it takes individuals and turns them into interchangeable, indistinguishable parts. It is what happens to those parts when they go to war that is so horrifying.

And it is here where the writer's voice is most essential, and here where the voice of the writer who has been to war is most precious.

One of the greatest of those voices is that of Wilfred Owen, whose poems, written on the front during WWI, highlight the anonymity of war in order to fight against it. His "Anthem for Doomed Youth" begins with the stark question, "What passing bells for those who die as cattle?" and his concern throughout his verse is with the tragedy of these individual men, sent to die en masse. The movement of his most famous poem, "Dulce et Decorum Est" is from a wide angle view of a troupe of soldiers marching "Bent double, like old beggars under sacks, / Knock-kneed, coughing like hags, we cursed through sludge" to an individualized close-up of one soldier caught without a mask during a gas attack.

> But someone still was yelling out and stumbling
> And flound'ring like a man in fire or lime.—
> Dim through the misty panes and thick green light,
> As under a green sea, I saw him drowning.
>
> In all my dreams before my helpless sight,
> He plunges at me, guttering, choking, drowning.

From here, Owen turns to the reader to say, "If you could see what I have seen, and hear what I have heard, you would not think so much of the glories of war." And thus, through his art, the anonymous soldier is made individual, and then his death is made painfully personal.

Yeats does something similar in his poem "Easter 1916" which closes with a catalogue of those lost in the Easter uprising.

> I write it out in a verse—
> MacDonagh and MacBride
> And Connolly and Pearse
> Now and in time to be,
> Wherever green is worn,
> Are changed, changed utterly:
> A terrible beauty is born.

The simple listing of the names of the dead acknowledges that lives lost are *lives* that were lost, not mere body counts. And literature insists that we attend to those lives and to those voices. What, we wonder, was the name of the Boy in *Henry V*?

While Yeats finds beauty, though a terrible one, in the loss of those individuals, Israeli poet Yehuda Amichai finds nothing but despair.

> The diameter of the bomb was thirty centimeters
> and the diameter of its effective range about seven meters,
> with four dead and eleven wounded.
> And around these, in a larger circle
> of pain and time, two hospitals are scattered
> and one graveyard. But the young woman
> who was buried in the city she came from,
> at a distance of more than a hundred kilometers,
> enlarges the circle considerably,
> and the solitary man mourning her death
> at the distant shores of a country far across the sea
> includes the entire world in the circle.
> And I won't even mention the crying of orphans
> that reaches up to the throne of God and
> beyond, making a circle with no end and no God.

Just as Owen's "Dulce et Decorum Est" focuses in on increasingly intimate views of a gas attack and then demands that the reader consider what it means to him or her, Amichai insists that his readers consider what a small bomb means when we begin to understand the concentric circles of its influence. The bomb may have killed only four, but its effects reach "up to the throne of God and beyond."

There is value in studying the large numbers of war. We need to know how much we spend, how many soldiers we lose, how many civilians are killed. But we also need to remember that the large numbers, no matter how much they can tell us, do not tell us everything. To look only at what Amy Lowell referred to as "the pattern called a war" obscures the details that make up that pattern and allows us to forget about the lives of the individuals who provide those details.

Many writers have commented on the feeling of futility that arises from being a writer in wartime, when people want news and not art. Pablo Neruda offers a famously bitter explanation for why he is not writing much, or well, during war time:

> You will ask: why doesn't his poetry
> Speak to us of dreams, of leaves
> of the great volcanoes of his native land?
>
> Come and see the blood in the streets,
> come and see
> the blood in the streets,
> come and see the blood
> in the streets!

In time of war, he suggests, what is there to say but "come and see the blood in the streets"? And when that is all there is to say, what use is poetry?

But Auden reminds us that the writer's voice can and must be used to personalize the blood in the streets and to make it matter. It's not merely blood; it's *someone's* blood. The voice of the individual must be used to defend the value of the individual against the folded lies of war.

> All I have is a voice
> To undo the folded lie,
> The romantic lie in the brain
> Of the sensual man-in-the-street
> And the lie of Authority
> Whose buildings grope the sky:
> There is no such thing as the State
> And no one exists alone;
> Hunger allows no choice
> To the citizen or the police;
> We must love one another or die.

12

THE WAR PRAYER

By Mark Twain

> Samuel Langhorne Clemens, better known by his pen name of Mark Twain, was one of the greatest writers in American history. His books include *The Adventures of Tom Sawyer* and *Adventures of Huckleberry Finn*.

It was a time of great and exalting excitement. The country was up in arms, the war was on, in every breast burned the holy fire of patriotism; the drums were beating, the bands playing, the toy pistols popping, the bunched firecrackers hissing and spluttering; on every hand and far down the receding and fading spread of roofs and balconies a fluttering wilderness of flags flashed in the sun; daily the young volunteers marched down the wide avenue gay and fine in their new uniforms, the proud fathers and mothers and sisters and sweethearts cheering them with voices choked with happy emotion as they swung by; nightly the packed mass meetings listened, panting, to patriot oratory which stirred the deepest deeps of their hearts, and which they interrupted at briefest intervals with cyclones of applause, the tears running down their cheeks the while; in the churches the pastors preached devotion to flag and country, and invoked the God of Battles beseeching His aid in our good cause in outpourings of fervid eloquence which moved every listener.

It was indeed a glad and gracious time, and the half dozen rash spirits that ventured to disapprove of the war and cast a doubt upon its righteousness straightway got such a stern and angry warning that for their personal safety's sake they quickly shrank out of sight and offended no more in that way.

Sunday morning came—next day the battalions would leave for the front; the church was filled; the volunteers were there, their young faces alight with martial dreams—visions of the stern advance, the gathering momentum, the rushing charge, the flashing sabers, the flight of the foe, the tumult, the enveloping smoke, the fierce pursuit, the surrender!

Then home from the war, bronzed heroes, welcomed, adored, submerged in golden seas of glory! With the volunteers sat their dear ones, proud, happy, and envied by the neighbors and friends who had no sons and brothers to send forth to the field of honor, there to win for the flag, or, failing, die the noblest of noble deaths. The service proceeded; a war chapter from the Old Testament was read; the first prayer was said; it was followed by an organ burst that shook the building, and with one impulse the house rose, with glowing eyes and beating hearts, and poured out that tremendous invocation:

God the all-terrible! Thou who ordainest, Thunder thy clarion and lightning thy sword!

Then came the "long" prayer. None could remember the like of it for passionate pleading and moving and beautiful language. The burden of its supplication was, that an ever-merciful and benignant Father of us all would watch over our noble young soldiers, and aid, comfort, and encourage them in their patriotic work; bless them, shield them in the day of battle and the hour of peril, bear them in His mighty hand, make them strong and confident, invincible in the bloody onset; help them crush the foe, grant to them and to their flag and country imperishable honor and glory—

An aged stranger entered and moved with slow and noiseless step up the main aisle, his eyes fixed upon the minister, his long body clothed in a robe that reached to his feet, his head bare, his white hair descending in a frothy cataract to his shoulders, his seamy face unnaturally pale, pale even to ghastliness. With all eyes following him and wondering, he made his silent way; without pausing, he ascended to the preacher's side and stood there waiting. With shut lids the preacher, unconscious of his presence, continued his moving prayer, and at last finished it with the words, uttered in fervent appeal, "Bless our arms, grant us the victory, O Lord and God, Father and Protector of our land and flag!"

The stranger touched his arm, motioned him to step aside—which the startled minister did—and took his place. During some moments he surveyed the spellbound audience with solemn eyes, in which burned an uncanny light; then in a deep voice he said:

"I come from the Throne—bearing a message from Almighty God!" The words smote the house with a shock; if the stranger perceived it he gave no attention. "He has heard the prayer of His servant your shepherd, and will grant it if such be your desire after I, His messenger, shall have explained to you its import—that is to say, its full import. For it is like unto many of the prayers of men, in that it asks for more than he who utters it is aware of—except he pause and think.

"God's servant and yours has prayed his prayer. Has he paused and taken thought? Is it one prayer? No, it is two—one uttered, and the other not. Both have reached the ear of Him who heareth all supplications, the spoken and the unspoken. Ponder this—keep it in mind. If you would beseech a blessing upon yourself, beware! lest without intent you invoke a curse upon your neighbor at the same time. If you pray for the blessing of rain on your crop which needs it, by that act you are possibly praying for a curse on some neighbor's crop which may not need rain and can be injured by it.

"You have heard your servant's prayer—the uttered part of it. I am commissioned by God to put into words the other part of it—that part which the pastor—and also you in your hearts—fervently prayed silently. And ignorantly and unthinkingly? God grant that it was so! You heard the words 'Grant us the victory, O Lord our God!' That is sufficient. The whole of the uttered prayer is compact into those pregnant words. Elaborations were not necessary. When you have prayed for victory you have prayed for many unmentioned results which follow victory—must follow it, cannot help but follow it. Upon the listening spirit of God fell also the unspoken part of the prayer. He commandeth me to put it into words. Listen!

"Lord our Father, our young patriots, idols of our hearts, go forth into battle—be Thou near them! With them—in spirit—we also go forth from the sweet peace of our beloved firesides to smite the foe. O Lord our God, help us tear their soldiers to bloody shreds with our shells; help us to cover their smiling fields with the pale forms of their patriot dead; help us to drown the thunder of the guns with the shrieks of their wounded, writhing in pain; help us to lay waste their humble homes with a hurricane of fire; help us to wring the hearts of their unoffending widows with unavailing grief; help us to turn them out roofless with their little children to wander unfriended in the wastes of their desolated land in rags and hunger and thirst, sports of the sun flames of summer and the icy winds of winter, broken in spirit, worn with travail, imploring thee for the refuge of the grave and denied it—

"For our sakes who adore Thee, Lord, blast their hopes, blight their lives, protract their bitter pilgrimmage, make heavy their steps, water their way with their tears, stain the white snow with the blood of their wounded feet!

"We ask it, in the spirit of love, of Him Who is the Source of Love, and Who is the ever-faithful refuge and friend of all that are sore beset and seek His aid with humble and contrite hearts. Amen."

(After a pause.) "Ye have prayed it; if ye still desire it, speak! The messenger of the Most High waits."

It was believed afterward that the man was a lunatic, because there was no sense in what he said.

13

DULCE ET DECORUM EST

By Wilfred Owen

Wilfred Owen was an English poet and soldier. He was killed in action on November 4, 1918, one week before the Armistice that ended the First World War was signed.

Bent double, like old beggars under sacks,
Knock-kneed, coughing like hags, we cursed through sludge,
Till on the haunting flares we turned our backs
And towards our distant rest began to trudge.
Men marched asleep. Many had lost their boots
But limped on, blood-shod. All went lame; all blind;
Drunk with fatigue; deaf even to the hoots
Of tired, outstripped Five-Nines that dropped behind.
Gas! Gas! Quick, boys!—An ecstasy of fumbling,
Fitting the clumsy helmets just in time;
But someone still was yelling out and stumbling,
And flound'ring like a man in fire or lime . . .
Dim, through the misty panes and thick green light,
As under a green sea, I saw him drowning.
In all my dreams, before my helpless sight,
He plunges at me, guttering, choking, drowning.
If in some smothering dreams you too could pace
Behind the wagon that we flung him in,
And watch the white eyes writhing in his face,
His hanging face, like a devil's sick of sin;

If you could hear, at every jolt, the blood
Come gargling from the froth-corrupted lungs,
Obscene as cancer, bitter as the cud
Of vile, incurable sores on innocent tongues,
My friend, you would not tell with such high zest
To children ardent for some desperate glory,
The old Lie; Dulce et Decorum est
Pro patria mori.

14

PARABLE OF THE OLD MAN AND THE YOUNG

By Wilfred Owen

Wilfred Owen was an English poet and soldier. He was killed in action on November 4, 1918, one week before the Armistice that ended the First World War was signed.

So Abram rose, and clave the wood, and went,
And took the fire with him, and a knife.
And as they sojourned both of them together,
Isaac the first-born spake and said, My Father,
Behold the preparations, fire and iron,
But where the lamb for this burnt-offering?
Then Abram bound the youth with belts and straps,
and builded parapets and trenches there,
And stretchèd forth the knife to slay his son.
When lo! an angel called him out of heaven,
Saying, Lay not thy hand upon the lad,
Neither do anything to him. Behold,
A ram, caught in a thicket by its horns;
Offer the Ram of Pride instead of him.

But the old man would not so, but slew his son,
And half the seed of Europe, one by one.

15

PEACE BEGINS WITH YOU

By Cathy Reisenwitz

> What can you, the reader of this book, do to make the world more peaceful? How can you make a difference? What are the steps you can take and what resources are available to you? Cathy Reisenwitz is an editor at *Young Voices* and works with Students For Liberty. Her writing on politics and culture has appeared in such publications as *Forbes*, the *Chicago Tribune*, *Reason*, *VICE Motherboard*, and the *Washington Examiner*.

War surrounds us, yet hides itself. Whereas at one time wars had discrete beginnings and ends, we now live in a state of perpetual conflict. Because ongoing wars are being waged, not on foreign states, but on such abstractions as "drugs" and "terror," it is not possible to know whether victory has ever been won. Terror is a tactic and drugs are commodities; they cannot be "defeated" like traditional enemies. Thus, the wars against them are perpetual.

Wars destroy lives but also undermine the rule of law and our civil liberties, the very institutions that make civil society possible. Secret drone programs are used to execute designated targets, without any form of trial. Massive spying programs are initiated and justified as necessary to prosecute wars on enemies real and imagined. Armed forces deploy to "failed states," frequently merely destabilizing the local equilibria even more. Armed force is used to destabilize political systems and create chaos, in order to justify armed intervention and annexation. Local "peace officers" are increasingly transformed into military assault units who increasingly treat local citizens more like enemies on the battlefield.

Add to those instances of state violence the invasions of Iraq and Afghanistan, Chechnya, Georgia, and Crimea, the armed conflicts in Libya and Syria, Somalia and Darfur, and numerous other conflict countries and one realizes that most Millennials have never known a time of peace. We have grown up with a world at war, whether declared or undeclared, unilateral or multilateral. How can we possibly advocate for that unknown ideal: peace?

Yet the general trend over centuries has been away from war. The daily lives of ever more people have been more peaceful than those of earlier generations. Global commerce and communication, the instruments of peace, have brought forth the most globally conscious generation yet—true citizens of the world.

The likelihood of dying from violence has declined for most people in most places, but campaigns of state-organized violence have also become virtually perpetual for the citizens of many countries. The victims of such perpetual wars are often hidden from public view: innocent bystanders killed in drone strikes; victims of the gang and police violence that accompanies prohibition (the "drug war") and lawless "black markets"; combatants and noncombatants alike killed in direct military conflicts; and hardest of all victims for most people to see, liberty, limited government, and the rule of law.

So what can our generation do to protect peace? Three steps: *Learn. Amplify. Organize.*

Learn

Those who clamor for war count on an uninformed, complacent, trusting populace. Economic fallacies, such as the ruse that wars "stimulate the economy," when combined with misinformation, outright deception, and appeals to a false patriotism that demonizes those who dare to ask questions can stampede people into war or lull them into complacency about what their governments are doing. Mere statements of intention are offered as substitutes for reasonable accounts of the likely consequences of the use of armed force. The very idea that there might be unintended consequences or additional risks is dismissed out of hand. Being informed, understanding incentives, risks and tradeoffs, digging for the facts, and even being suspicious of the intentions of politicians and willing to challenge them are all important to the maintenance of peace. This book is a good start, but there is much more to be done for those who wish to work for peace.

We must educate ourselves on foreign affairs and learn the history of military interventionism, especially as seen from the perspective of its victims. War is a serious matter and demands of us our attention to the facts, to the possibility of unintended consequences, to the full costs, and to the likely effects on life, liberty, and the pursuit of happiness.

A good place to start, after finishing the essays in this book, is with the "Suggestions for Further Reading" at the end of this volume. For more detailed "policy-oriented" information and analysis, an excellent source is www.cato.org/foreign-policy-national-security. In countries with open access to the Internet, search engines (when coupled with a healthy skepticism about sources) are also invaluable sources of information.

Amplify
Sometimes, all it takes to induce people to speak up for peace is for them to hear someone else do it first. You can be that first person. When you hear someone express support for violence, make the case for peace and voluntarism. That may be in personal conversation (where it's best to produce reasons, rather than anger, to help those around you to think past the slogans and to see the horror, the waste, and the suffering caused by violence), or on Facebook or other social media, or at public meetings, or via letters to the editor, radio call-ins, debates, or articles in your student newspaper. You'll generally find that you're not alone and that your voice will be amplified by the voices of others who would otherwise have remained silent.

A key insight of the great peace advocate Frédéric Bastiat was that policies of government have not only "seen" effects, but "unseen" effects, as well. What did *not* happen because the politicians ordered something done? Jeeps and tanks *are* built for war, meaning that cars and tractors *are not*. Jobs are *created* in armaments industries, meaning that they are *destroyed* in peaceful enterprises. Every choice has a cost, something given up, something that doesn't happen, something that's not seen. War is no different. It's also a choice and all choices entail costs. Helping people to appreciate the costs, to see the "unseen," is a great step toward undercutting foolish and reckless moves toward war.

You can express your views to elected representatives if you live in a country with at least some degree of responsive government. Each well-stated personalized communication tells the politician that a lot more people think as you do. They generally pay attention to such communications, far more than most people think. (Angry denunciations tend to be ignored.)

If you see online articles or studies that you think make good arguments for peace, you should share them via Twitter, Facebook, VK, your blog, or other media. When others comment on them, you should respond rationally and help to engage both their minds and their hearts for peace. In every interaction, it's best to be persuasive, rather than angry. It's best to convince, rather than to denounce. The point is not to vent our anger, but to convince others to join us on the road to peace.

In short, you can share your enthusiasm for peace, love, and liberty. (In fact, you can get more copies of this book and share them with family members, friends, or classmates—even, if you're feeling a bit bold, with professors.)

Organize

If you're in college, find a Students For Liberty chapter and become active. It's easy; it's rewarding; and you'll meet friends who share your commitment to peace, love, and liberty. You can find out how to join a chapter or start a chapter at studentsforliberty.org. Or check out the Atlas Network Global Directory (http://AtlasNetwork.org/) to find organizations that stand up for the reforms that create peaceful societies.

Then, start organizing for peace. Others are doing it and so can you. Here are just a few recent examples, drawn from the United States (where I live) and elsewhere:

In October 2012, the Michigan State University College Libertarians created a Civil Liberties graveyard. They created fake tombstones, each representing a freedom ("privacy," "free speech," "habeas corpus," and "religious freedom") that has fallen or is likely to fall victim to war. They placed the tombstones at a main campus intersection, where they were sure to attract attention. There they handed out educational material and recruited new members to their group.

In March 2012, the Slippery Rock University Young Americans for Liberty helped students to understand the magnitude of US fatalities in the Iraq and Afghanistan wars during their "Decade of War" event on campus. They filled the quad with US flags, each one representing two American fatalities in the last decade of war. They also constructed a "Free Speech Wall" located among the flags for students to share their thoughts on war. Thousands upon thousands of students walked by the display every day for a week. The event enabled the group to talk to fellow students about the implications of the wars as well as introduce them to their club by tabling in front of the display and handing out literature on liberty.

In April 2013, the University of Florida College Libertarians organized an "Anti-Drone Week of Action." It brought together groups from across the political spectrum to protest the government's use of drones, as well as decisions made by the university that promoted the militarized use of drones. They also created a free speech wall featuring a painting of a missile-bearing drone and set out tables on high traffic areas of campus featuring a "Pin the Drone on the Warzone" display that allowed students to see where drones are being deployed.

In March 2014, attendees at the European Students For Liberty conference in Berlin marched to the Russian Embassy to protest the Kremlin's invasion of Ukraine and the ongoing annexation of Crimea. The group included students from both Russia and Ukraine who were united in opposing the armed invasion of one country by another.

In countries where speech is more thoroughly controlled or suppressed by governments, such work may be harder to carry out, but students for peace still manage to make their voices heard. In Russia,

Students For Liberty activists marched in Moscow, St. Petersburg, and other cities against intervening militarily in Ukraine (and were arrested for their bravery). In India and Pakistan, Students For Liberty have promoted freedom of trade to substitute peace and friendship for the wars, skirmishes, and hostility that have characterized too much of their history. Members of Students For Liberty in Africa have worked to promote civil peace in a number of countries that have suffered from violent conflict. The same is true in Latin America, where Students For Liberty activists in Venezuela, Guatemala, El Salvador, and elsewhere are working for peace.

The fact is that you—the person reading this essay—can make a difference. You can join others and actively promote peace. If there is not currently a group or a movement to join, you can start one. Each group and each movement was started by someone. Let that someone be you.

Make the Difference: Choose Peace

You've educated yourself by reading this book. There's more you can learn, of course, but you've already taken a huge step toward peace. You have an educated voice that you can deploy for peace. Let your voice be heard and you'll find that you're not alone, that others will join their voices to yours and amplify the message of peace. Organize with others to demonstrate your support for peace. When you are old and gray, will you be able to say, "I took my stand for peace"?

SUGGESTIONS FOR FURTHER READING

Because war has played such a central role in human history, there is a vast literature on the topic, celebrating, describing, and condemning it. The footnotes in this volume offer guides to additional reading and study. What follow are a few of the more important titles that consider the issues of war and peace from the perspective of those who prize liberty, voluntary cooperative activity, and mutual prosperity over submission, command, and glorious violence.

"The Law," "The State," and Other Political Writings, 1843–1850, by Frédéric Bastiat (Indianapolis: Liberty Fund, 2012), includes powerful writings on the nature of war, plunder, and statism by one of the greatest economic writers of the nineteenth century. Bastiat explains how government can become predatory and destructive, rather than protective. (Other works by Bastiat, including other works in the Liberty Fund series, also are worth reading.)

The Libertarian Reader: Classic and Contemporary Writings from Lao Tzu to Milton Friedman, ed. by David Boaz (New York: The Free Press, 1997; updated edition forthcoming 2015), offers not only an overview of libertarian thought from ancient to modern times, but a well organized section on "Peace and International Harmony" that includes classic essays on peace.

Depression, War, and Cold War: Studies in Political Economy, by Robert Higgs (Oxford: Oxford University Press, 2006), offers a thorough and evidence-based debunking of the myth that the Second World War "got the economy out of depression" and provides careful studies of the political and economic impact of war and of the role of defense contractors in formulation of public policy, among other topics.

On War and Morality, by Robert Holmes (Princeton; Princeton University Press, 1989), offers a useful look at the moral issues involved in war and challenges us to think through the full consequences of waging war.

Terror, Security, and Money: Balancing the Risks, Benefits, and Costs of Homeland Security, by John Mueller and Mark G. Stewart (Oxford: Oxford University Press, 2011), offers a different (and more rational) approach to considering risks and responses. This book is especially useful as a guide to cost-benefit analysis and rational risk management.

A History of Force: Exploring the worldwide movement against habits of coercion, bloodshed, and mayhem by James L. Payne (Sandpoint, Idaho: Lytton Publishing Co., 2004), offers a pioneering look at the ways in which violence and brutality have been replaced over time by cooperation and civil society.

The Better Angels of Our Nature: A History of Violence and Humanity by Steven Pinker (London: Penguin Books, 2011), provides data and analysis on "The Long Peace" and compares possible explanations of the decline in violence. Pinker combines statistics on violence, social history, political theory, and psychology into a scholarly tour de force of great importance.

"The Conquest of the United States by Spain" by William Graham Sumner (1898) (Indianapolis: Liberty Fund, 2013), offers the classic statement of the contrast between a republic and an empire.

There is a vast and growing online library of classic works in the classical liberal/libertarian tradition in the Online Library of Liberty, at http://oll.libertyfund.org.

About the Editor
Tom G. Palmer

Dr. Tom G. Palmer is executive vice president for international programs at the Atlas Network. He oversees the work of teams working around the world to advance the principles of classical liberalism and works with a global network of think tanks and research institutes. Dr. Palmer is a senior fellow of the Cato Institute, where he was formerly vice president for international programs and director of the Center for the Promotion of Human Rights.

He was an H. B. Earhart Fellow at Hertford College, Oxford University, and a vice president of the Institute for Humane Studies at George Mason University. He is a member of the board of advisors of Students For Liberty. He has published reviews and articles on politics and morality in scholarly journals such as the *Harvard Journal of Law and Public Policy*, *Ethics*, *Critical Review*, and *Constitutional Political Economy*, as well as in publications such as *Slate*, the *Wall Street Journal*, the *New York Times*, *Die Welt*, *Al Hayat*, *Caixing*, the *Washington Post*, and *The Spectator of London*.

He received his BA in liberal arts from St. Johns College in Annapolis, Maryland; his MA in philosophy from The Catholic University of America, Washington, DC; and his doctorate in politics from Oxford University. His scholarship has been published in books from Princeton University Press, Cambridge University Press, Routledge, and other academic publishers. He is the author of *Realizing Freedom: Libertarian Theory, History, and Practice* (expanded edition published in 2014); the editor of *The Morality of Capitalism*, published in 2011, *After the Welfare State*, published in 2012, and *Why Liberty*, published in 2013.

NOTES

1   Nelson Mandela, *Long Walk to Freedom* (New York: Little, Brown and Company, 1995) p. 622.

2   More information on libertarian ideas can be found in another book in this series, *Why Liberty*, Tom G. Palmer, ed. (Ottawa, Ill.: Jameson Books, 2013).

3   Cicero, *On Duties* (Cambridge: Cambridge University Press, 1991), Book III, pp. 109–10.

4   James Madison, *The Writings of James Madison, comprising his Public Papers and his Private Correspondence, including his numerous letters and documents now for the first time printed*, ed. Gaillard Hunt (New York: G.P. Putnam's Sons, 1900). Vol. 6. Chapter: Universal Peace, Originally published in *The National Gazette*, February 2, 1792. Accessed from http://oll.libertyfund.org/title/1941/124396 on 2014-02-16.

5   Colin Powell, *My American Journey* (1996; revised ed., New York: Ballantine Books, 2003), p. 576.

6   "US Policy on Iraq draws fire in Ohio," CNN Special Report, "The Standoff with Iraq," February 18, 1998, accessed at http://edition.cnn.com/WORLD/9802/18/town.meeting.folo/. When Hillary Clinton, the wife of the president who preceded Bush and a member of the U.S. Senate when the vote was cast, had to defend her vote to authorize military force as a candidate for the Democratic Party nomination for president in 2006, she stated, "Obviously, if we knew then what we know now, there wouldn't have been a vote and I certainly wouldn't have voted that way." Toby Harnden, "Clinton shifts over Iraq as Obama threatens," *The Telegraph*, December 20, 2006, available at http://www.telegraph.co.uk/news/worldnews/1537474/Clinton-shifts-over-Iraq-as-Obama-threatens.html (Perhaps she should have thought about whether things might turn out badly before casting her vote, or even listened to the many voices at the time warning about the looming catastrophe of the proposed war.)

7   Iraq Body Count Project, http://www.iraqbodycount.org/database/.

8   Linda J. Bilmes, "The Financial Legacy of Iraq and Afghanistan: How Wartime Spending Decisions Will Constrain Future National Security Budgets," Harvard Kennedy School Faculty Research Working Paper Series, March 2013, RWP-13-006.

9   The philosophical arguments are well canvassed in Richard Tuck, *The Rights of War and Peace: Political Thought and the International Order from Grotius to Kant* (Oxford: Oxford University Press, 1999). The relevant treaties and other legal documents are collected in Adam Roberts and Richard Guelff, eds., *Documents on the Laws of War* (Oxford: Oxford University Press, 2001).

10   Robert Holmes, *On War and Morality* (Princeton; Princeton University Press, 1989), pp 178–79.

11   Robert Holmes, *ibid.*, p. 179.

12   Robert Holmes, *ibid.*, p. 180. Holmes adds, "So given that one can know to a virtual certainty that he commits himself to doing these things in going to war, fully to justify going to war requires justifying these acts as well. A necessary condition of the justifiable pursuit of *any* objectives in war, by *any means* whatever (hence a necessary condition of the satisfaction of the criteria of both *jus ad bellum* and *jus in bello*), is that one can be justified in engaging in such killing and violence in the first place."

13   Quoted, with full video link, in Glenn Greenwald, "Joe Klein's socio-pathic defense of drone killings of children," *The Guardian*, October 23, 2012, available at http://www.theguardian.com/commentisfree/2012/oct/23/klein-drones-morning-joe?newsfeed=true.

14   Randolph Bourne, "The State," in Randolph Bourne, *The Radical Will: Selected Writings 1911–1918* (Berkeley: University of California Press, 1992), pp. 355–95, p. 360.

15   Robert Higgs, *Crisis and Leviathan: Critical Episodes in the Growth of American Government* (Oxford: Oxford University Press, 1987), p. 73.

16   Thomas Paine, *The Rights of Man, Part I*, in Paine, *Political Writings*, ed. by Bruce Kuklick (Cambridge: Cambridge University Press, 1989), p. 86.

17   Margaret Levi, *Of Rule and Revenue* (Berkeley: University of California Press, 1988), p. 105.

18   William Shakespeare, *Henry IV, Part II*, Act IV, Scene 5.

19   Plutarch, *Plutarch's Lives. The Translation called Dryden's*. Corrected from the Greek and Revised by A.H. Clough, in 5 volumes (Boston: Little Brown and Co., 1906). Vol. 4, Chapter, "Cato the Younger." Accessed from http://oll.libertyfund.org/title/1774/93963 on 2014-02-22.

20   Julius Caesar (2004-01-01). *"De Bello Gallico" and Other*

Commentaries, Book IV, 14–15 (Kindle Locations 1374–80). Public Domain Books. Kindle Edition.

21   Reading accounts of the orgy of violence in the period is a draining experience. The Axis powers (and Germany's Soviet ally) initiated the war and some of the Axis military and political leaders were justly punished, but they were not the only source of carnage. Most of the crimes went completely unpunished, as is always the case with wars.

22   Unknown author, "Of the Origin of Homer and Hesiod, and of their Contest," in *Hesiod, the Homeric Hymns, and Homerica*, trans. by Hugh E. G. Evelyn-White (Cambridge, Ma.: Harvard University Press, 1914), pp. 585–87.

23   Benjamin Constant, "The Spirit of Conquest and Usurpation and their Relation to European Civilization," in *Constant, Political Writings*, Biancamaria Fontana, ed. (Cambridge: Cambridge University Press, 1988), p. 82.

24   Jean-Baptiste Say, *A Treatise on Political Economy*, (Philadelphia: Lippincot, Grambo & Co.), Book III, chapter 6, §. 51. Accessed online: http://www.econlib.org/library/Say/sayT39.html#Bk.III,Ch.VI.

25   Say, *Treatise*, Book III, chapter 6, §. 54. http://www.econlib.org/library/Say/sayT39.html#Bk.III,Ch.VI.

26   Jean-Baptiste Say, *Catéchisme d'économie politique* (Paris: Guillaumin et Cie, libraries, Sixième edition, 1881), p. 9. "Produire, c'est donner de la valeur aux choses en leur donnant de l'utilité." This sentence does not appear in the English edition.

27   Say also explained the importance of peaceful competition among rival producers and consumers. Market competition is a *process* that is driven by entrepreneurial innovation; prices act as signals that guide economic players to opportunities for gain. It's also a learning process, proceeding through trial and error, which brings new and improved products and other benefits to consumers. The essential condition for competition is freedom of entry, for which reason Say was so critical of privileged guilds, state-granted concessions, royally chartered corporations, and the like, which restricted markets and created monopolies.

28   Say, *Treatise*, Book I, chap. 15, §. 3. http://www.econlib.org/library/Say/sayT15.html#Bk.I,Ch.XV.

29   Adam Smith, *An Inquiry into the Nature and Causes of the Wealth of Nations* (Indianapolis: Liberty Fund, 1979), Book I, Chap. 3, p. 31.

30   Say, *Treatise*, Book I, chap. 15, §. 15.

31 *Ibid.*, §. 9.

32 *Ibid.*, §. 4.

33 *Ibid.*, §. 16.

34 *Ibid.*, §. 17.

35 *Ibid.*, §. 18.

36 Jean-Baptiste Say, *Letters to Mr. Malthus, on Several Subjects of Political Economy, and on the Cause of the Stagnation of Commerce. To Which is added, A Catechism of Political Economy, or Familiar Conversations on the Manner in which Wealth is Produced, Distributed, and Consumed in Society,* trans. John Richter (London: Sherwood, Neely, and Jones, 1821). Letter 1: http://oll.libertyfund.org/index.php?option=com_staticxt&staticfile=show.php%3Ftitle=1795&layout=html#chapter_99253.

37 Say, *Letters to Mr. Malthus*, Letter 1.

38 Say, *Treatise*, Book I, Chapter XVII, §. 55. http://www.econlib.org/library/Say/sayT17.html#Bk.I,Ch.XVII

39 Say, *Treatise*, Book I, Chap 11, Note 7. http://www.econlib.org/library/Say/sayT11.html#Bk.I,Ch.XI.

40 Say, *Treatise*, Book I, chap. 14, §. 9. The disaster of such violent governments is that people "withdraw a part of their property from the greedy eyes of power: and value can never be invisible, without being inactive" (Say, *Treatise*, Book I, chap. 14, §. 9). http://www.econlib.org/library/Say/sayT14.html.

41 Say, *Treatise*, Book III, chapter 6, §. 54. http://www.econlib.org/library/Say/sayT39.html#Bk.III,Ch.VI.

42 See, for example, Samuel P. Huntington. *The Third Wave: Democratization in the Late Twentieth Century* (Norman, OK: University of Oklahoma Press, 1991).

43 Polity data are an extremely widely used measure of democracy. See Keith Jaggers and Ted Robert Gurr, "Transitions to Democracy: Tracking Democracy's 'Third Wave' with the Polity III Data," *Journal of Peace Research* 32(4) 1995:469–82.

44 Figure 1 uses trade data provided by the World Bank. Figure 2 is from Erik Gartzke and Alex Weisiger, "Under Construction: Development, Democracy, and Difference as Determinants of the Systemic Liberal Peace," *International Studies Quarterly* 58(1) 2014: 130–45.

45 Thomas C. Schelling, *Arms and Influence* (New Haven: Yale University Press, 1966), p. 99.

46 Baron de Montesquieu *Spirit of the Laws* (Cambridge: Cambridge University Press, 1989[1748]); Adam Smith *An Inquiry into the*

Nature and Causes of the Wealth of Nations (Chicago: University of Chicago Press, 1976[1776]); Thomas Paine *Common Sense* (New York: Penguin, 1986[1776]); Immanuel Kant *Perpetual Peace: A Philosophical Essay* (New York: Garland, 1972[1795]); Richard Cobden *Political Writings* (London: T. Fisher Unwin, 1903[1867]); Norman Angell *The Great Illusion* (New York: Putnam, 1933). Richard Rosecrance *The Rise of the Trading State: Commerce and Conquest in the Modern World* (New York: Basic Books, 1985); Bruce Russett *Grasping the Democratic Peace: Principles for a Post-Cold War World* (Princeton: Princeton University Press, 1993); Michael Doyle Ways of War and Peace: *Realism, Liberalism and Socialism* (New York: Norton, 1997).

47   Steven Pinker *The Better Angels of our Nature: Why Violence has Declined* (New York: Viking Press, 2011); Joshua S. Goldstein, *Winning the War on War: The Decline of Armed Conflict Worldwide* (New York: Dutton, 2011); The global nature of the decline in war is more tenuous. The relationship (between modernity and peace) is strongest among developed nations.

48   Peter Brecke "Violent Conflicts 1400 AD to the Present in Different Regions of the World." Paper presented at the Annual Meetings of the Peace Science Society (International). Results for other regions (Africa, Asia, the Americas) are both shorter in duration and less definitive.

49   Cioffi-Revilla, Claudio. 2004. "The Next Record-Setting War in the Global Setting: A Long-Term Analysis." *Journal of the Washington Academy of Sciences* 90(2): 61–93. There is some debate among researchers about whether to weight measures of war intensity by population. In general, the risk to any individual of dying from warfare (intra- or inter-state) has declined.

50   See Bruce Russett, *Grasping the Democratic Peace: Principles for a Post-Cold War World* (Princeton, NJ: Princeton University Press, 1993) and Michael Doyle, *Ways of War and Peace: Realism, Liberalism, and Socialism* (New York: Norton, 1997).

51   Douglas North and Robert Thomas *The Rise of the Western World* (Cambridge: Cambridge University Press, 1973). Mancur Olson "Dictatorship, Democracy, and Development," 1993. *American Political Science Review* 87(3):567–76.

52   See, for example, Bruce Russett and John R. Oneal, *Triangulating Peace: Democracy, Interdependence, and International Organizations* (New York: Norton, 2001).

53   Trade leads to increased specialization which leads to higher productivity and increased real wages. Hal Varian *Microeconomic Analysis*, 3rd ed. (New York: W. W. Norton 1992).

54   Lance E. Davis and Robert A. Huttenback, with the assistance of Susan Gray Davis, *Mammon and the Pursuit of Empire: The Economics of British Imperialism,* abridged edition (Cambridge: Cambridge University Press, 1988), p. 267.

55   Frédéric Bastiat, "Peace and Freedom or the Republican Budget" (1849), in Frédéric Bastiat, *The Collected Works of Frédéric Bastiat. Vol. 2: The Law, The State, and Other Political Writings, 1843– 1850,* Jacques de Guenin, General Editor, (Indianapolis: Liberty Fund, 2012), pp. 282–327, p. 191. Available online at http://oll.libertyfund.org/index.php?option=com_staticxt&staticfile=show.php%3Ftitle=2450&Itemid=28.

56   Steven Pinker, *The Better Angels of Our Nature: A History of Violence and Humanity* (London: Penguin Books, 2011), p. xix.

57   James L. Payne, A *History of Force: Exploring the worldwide movement against habits of coercion, bloodshed, and mayhem* (Sandpoint, Idaho: Lytton Publishing Co., 2004), Steven Pinker, *op. cit.*

58   Huntington also revealed a disturbingly inadequate understanding of such terms as "competition" and "conflict": "Interestingly, if perplexingly, Americans endorse competition in American society between opinion groups, parties, branches of government, businesses. Why Americans believe that conflict is good within their own society and yet bad between societies is a fascinating question which, to the best of my knowledge, no one has seriously studied." Samuel Huntington, *The Clash of Civilizations and the Remaking of World Order* (New York: Simon & Schuster, 1997), p. 221. It seems not to have occurred to him that there may be reasons why no one had seriously studied such an intellectual confusion. The "checks and balances" among the branches of government and the competition among firms to attract customers are rather different from conflict "between societies."

59   Samuel Huntington, *ibid.,* p. 84.

60   Angus Maddison, *Contours of the World Economy, 1–2030 AD, Essays in Macro-Economic History* (Oxford: Oxford University Press, 2007), Data from Table A7, p. 382.

61   Jutta Bolt and Jan Luiten van Zanden, "The First Update of the Maddison Project: Re-Estimating Growth Before 1820," Maddison-Project Working Paper WP-4 (January 2013), available online at

http://www.ggdc.net/maddison/maddison-project/publications/
wp4.pdfa; database at http://www.ggdc.net/maddison/maddison-
project/data/mpd_2013-01.xlsx. In 2010 dollars the number was
much larger, of course, thanks to the inflationary policies of the
US Federal Reserve system. According to the World Bank (http://
data.worldbank.org/indicator/NY.GNP.PCAP.CD/countries/NL-
-XS?display=graph), in 2010 dollars, Dutch per capita GDP stood
at US$48,530.

62   Bolt and van Zanden database http://www.ggdc.net/maddison/
maddison-project/data/mpd_2013-01.xlsx.

63   Jean-Baptiste Say, *A Treatise on Political Economy*, trans. by C. R.
Prinsep and Clement C. Biddle (Philadelphia: Lippincott, Grambo
& Co., 1855), Book I, Chapter XV, "Of the Demand or Market
for Products," available from http://www.econlib.org/library/Say/
sayT15.html

64   Such a zero-sum view of the world would also mean that there
would never be trade at all, since people only trade if they expect
to benefit from it. Economic nationalism is incoherent from top
to bottom.

65   Adam Smith, *An Inquiry Into the Nature and Causes of the Wealth
of Nations,* ed. R. H. Campbell and A. S. Skinner, vol. II of the
Glasgow Edition of the Works and Correspondence of Adam Smith
(Indianapolis: Liberty Fund: 1981), IV: vii, "Of Colonies," p. 588.

66   Adam Smith, *An Inquiry Into the Nature and Causes of the Wealth
of Nations,* ed. R. H. Campbell and A. S. Skinner, vol. II of the
Glasgow Edition of the Works and Correspondence of Adam Smith
(Indianapolis: Liberty Fund: 1981). IV: viii, "Conclusion of the
Mercantile System," p. 661.

67   Smith's contemporary Jeremy Bentham was even more biting in his
characterization of foreign conquests. He declared that "All profit,
by conquest in any shape, I acknowledge to be no more than robbery: robbery, having murder for its instrument; both operating
upon the largest possible scale: robbery, committed by the ruling
few in the conquering nation, on the subject many in both nations:
robbery, of which by the expense of armament, the people of the
conquering nation are the first victims." Bentham regarded "all
such dominion, as no better than an instrument, a device, for the
accumulation of patronage and oppressive power, in the hands of
the ruling few in the dominating State, at the expense, and by the
sacrifice, of the interest and felicity, of the subject many, in both

States." Jeremy Bentham, "In International Dealings, Justice and Beneficience," in E.K. Bramsted and K.J. Melhuish, eds., *Western Liberalism: A History in Documents from Locke to Croce* (London: Longman, 1978), doc. 36, p. 353.

68 John Morley, *The Life of Richard Cobden* (London: T. Fisher Unwiin, 1903). Chapter XXXIII.: miscellaneous correspondence, 1859–60—paris—return to England. Accessed from http://oll.libertyfund.org/title/1742/90559/2050419 on 2014-01-02.

69 *Selected Speeches of the Rt. Hon. John Bright M.P. On Public Questions*, introduction by Joseph Sturge (London: J.M. Dent and Co., 1907), chapter XVI, Foreign Policy, Speech of October 29, 1858, Birmingham.

70 Lance E. Davis and Robert A. Huttenback, with the assistance of Susan Gray Davis, *Mammon and the Pursuit of Empire: The Economics of British Imperialism,* abridged edition (Cambridge: Cambridge University Press, 1988), p. 267.

71 The view that "the war got the US out of the Great Depression" is debunked quite thoroughly by the economic historian Robert Higgs in "Wartime Prosperity? A Reassessment of the U.S. Economy in the 1940s," *The Journal of Economic History*, Vol. 52, No. 1 (March 1992), and "From Central Planning to the Market: The American Transition, 945–47, *The Journal of Economic History*, Vol. 59, No. 3 (September 1999), both reprinted in revised form in Robert Higgs, *Depression, War, and Cold War: Studies in Political Economy* (Oxford: Oxford University Press, 2006), Chap. 3, pp. 61–80 and pp. 101–23.

72 "Et ainsi prévaut, malgré trop de douloureuses exceptions, cette loi d'harmonie et d'entente universelle qu'exprime si bien l'idée sublime de l'unité, de la fraternité de la race humaine. Le ressort de ce mouvement, c'est l'échange. Sans l'échange, les hommes et les peuples sont des frères égarés et devenus ennemis. Par l'échange, ils apprennent à se connaître et à s'aimer. Les intérêts les rapprochent, et le rapprochement les éclaire. Sans l'échange, chacun reste dans son coin, déshérité de l'univers entier, déchu un quelque sorte de la majeure partie de la création. Par l'échange, chacun retrouve ses titres en retrouvant ses biens, et rentre en partage de l'héritage inépuisable du père de famille. . . . Non-seulement elle [la doctrine de la prohibition et de la restriction] leur prêche l'isolement et le dénûment, mais elle les condamne à l'hostilité, à la haine." Frédéric Passy, *Leçons d'Économie politique faites à- Montpellier, 1860–1861* (Montpellier: Gras, 1861), p. 548.

73   William Graham Sumner, "The Conquest of the United States by Spain" (1898) (Indianapolis: Liberty Fund, 2013). Accessed from http://oll.libertyfund.org/title/2485 on 2014-02-03. See also David T. Beito and Linda Royster Beito, "Gold Democrats and the Decline of Classical Liberalism, 1896–1900," The *Independent Review*, vol. IV, no. 4 (Spring 2000), pp. 555–75, available online at http://www.independent.org/pdf/tir/tir_04_4_beito.pdf.

74   James Baker, "Confrontation in the Gulf: Excerpts from Baker Testimony on U.S. and Gulf," *New York Times*, September 5, 1990, available at http://www.nytimes.com/1990/09/05/world/confrontation-in-the-gulf-excerpts-from-baker-testimony-on-us-and-gulf.html.

75   Henry Kissinger, "U.S. Has Crossed Its Mideast Rubicon—and Cannot Afford to Lose," *Los Angeles Times*, August 19, 1990

76   William Niskanen and James Woolsey, "Should the United States Go to War against Iraq?" public debate at the Cato Institute, December 13, 2001, available at http://www.c-span.org/video/?167840-1/WarAgainst.

77   For the case of the First Gulf War, see David R. Henderson, "Do We Need to Go to War for Oil?," Cato *Institute Foreign Policy Briefing*, October 24, 1990, available at http://object.cato.org/sites/cato.org/files/pubs/pdf/fpb004.pdf. Henderson was formerly senior energy economist with the Council of Economic Advisers. He is an associate professor of economics at the Naval Postgraduate School. He calculated the costs of a price rise in oil due to a (very unlikely) substantial supply reduction that might be engineered by Saddam Hussein controlling oil from Iraq, Kuwait, Saudi Arabia, and the United Arab Emirates and found that the impact on the U.S. economy would be a fraction of the cost of U.S. military commitments to stop it. There simply was no economic case for the U.S. to project military power to the Persian Gulf.

78   See Eugene Gholz and Daryl G. Press, "Protecting 'The Prize': Oil and U.S. National Interest," *Security Studies*, Vol. 19, No. 3 (Fall 2010), pp. 453–85.

79   For one of many examples, "Derek Scissors, a resident scholar at the American Enterprise Institute who studies Chinese foreign investments, said Chinese companies tend to spend freely for assets. 'They overpay so the companies involved can sell the deal politically,' he said, and also because they have enormous pools of investment funds they want to spend. Some industry analysts agree that Chinese buyers may have overpaid in recent deals. Earlier this year, Sinochem

struck a deal with Pioneer Natural Resources Co for Permian Basin oil in Texas that was priced 40% higher than analysts had expected. Cnooc paid a 61% premium for Nexen, and Sinopec paid a 44% premium for oil-sands operator Daylight Energy." ("Chinese Energy Deals Focus on North America: State-Owned Firms Seek Secure Supplies, Advanced Technology," by Russell Gold and Chester Dawson, *Wall Street Journal*, October 25, 2013)

Not only is a higher price paid when the state purchases commodities abroad, but they are then provided at subsidized rates to favored state-owned enterprises in China, representing a double drain on the Chinese economy as a whole. As Hong Sheng and Nong Zhao of the Unirule Institute of Beijing note, "From 2001 to 2009, SOEs underpaid RMB 243.7 billion in resource taxes. Combined with coal, natural gas and other resources, SOEs underpaid a total of RMB 497.7 billion." Hong Sheng and Nong Zhao, *China's State-Owned Enterprises: Nature, Performance and Reform* (Singapore: World Scientific Publishing Company, 2012) (Kindle Edition Locations 242–43).

80   "'*Quand on est ami de la France, il faut penser aux entreprises françaises,*' aurait glissé M. Sarkozy, fin 2007, au président togolais Faure Gnassingbé (élu avec le soutien de la France) qui hésitait à concéder le port de Lomé au groupe Bolloré, selon *Le Canard enchaîné*." "La politique africaine de Nicolas Sarkozy tarde à rompre avec une certaine opacité," *Le Monde*, March 25, 2009, available at http://www.lemonde.fr/afrique/article/2009/03/25/la-politique-africaine-de-nicolas-sarkozy-tarde-a-rompre-avec-une-certaine-opacite_1172354_3212.html.

81   "Russia, with Belarus and Kazakhstan, its partners in the Customs Union, accounted for a third of all the world's protectionist steps in 2013, said the study by Global Trade Alert, or GTA, a leading independent trade monitoring service." "Russia Leads the World in Protectionist Trade Measures, Study Says," *Moscow Times*, January 12, 2014.

82   "Notre mission est de combattre cette fausse et dangereuse économie politique qui fait considerer la prospérité d'un peuple comme incompatible avec la prosperité d'un autre peuple, qui assimile le commerce à la conquête, le travail à la domination. Tant que ces idées subsisteront, jamais le monde ne pourra compter sur vingt-quatre heures de paix. Nous dirons plus, la paix serait une absurdité et une inconséquence." Frédéric Bastiat – M. de Noailles a la Chambre des Pairs, 24 Janvier 1847, in *Oeuvres Complètes de Frédéric Bastiat, Tome Deuxieme, Le*

Libre-Échange (Paris: Guillaumin et Cie., 1855), available at http://files.libertyfund.org/files/2343/Bastiat_Oeuvres_1561.02.pdf.

83   Jean-Baptiste Say, *A Treatise on Political Economy*, trans. by C. R. Prinsep and Clement C. Biddle (Philadelphia: Lippincott, Grambo & Co., 1855), Book I, Chapter XVII, "Of the Effect of Government Regulations Intended to Influence Production," available at http://oll.libertyfund.org/title/274/38004. The idea of the balance of trade is a pernicious fallacy that has been recognized as such for hundreds of years by economists, but which continues to enjoy popularity among people who haven't bothered to think it through. The great French economist Turgot, in his 1759 "Éloge de Gournay" about his teacher Vincent de Gournay, wrote that to defend mercantilist policies "is to forget that no operation of commerce can be otherwise than reciprocal, for to desire to sell everything to foreigners and to buy nothing from them is absurd." "Portrait of a Minister of Commerce, Éloge de Gournay," in W. Walker Stephens, ed., *The Life & Writings of Turgot* (1895; New York: Burt Franklin, 1971), p. 238.

84   Paul Krugman, "The Illusion of Conflict in International Trade," in Paul Krugman, *Pop Internationalism* (Cambridge, Mass.: The MIT Press, 1998), p. 84. Other essays in the book are well worth reading, including his very accessible "What Do Undergraduates Need to Know About Trade," pp. 116–25.

85   That is simply not possible, as the fundamental accounting identity "Savings – Investment = Exports – Imports" shows; if your imports are greater than your exports, your investment will be greater than your savings, so you are importing capital, and if your exports are greater than your imports, then your savings are greater than your investment, so you are exporting capital. For a thorough treatment of international trade, including its relationship to peace, see Donald J. Boudreaux, *Globalization* (Westport, CT: Greenwood Press, 2008).

86   Jean-Baptiste Say, *A Treatise on Political Economy*, Book I, Chapter XVII, "Of the Effect of Government Regulations Intended to Influence Production," available at http://oll.libertyfund.org/title/274/38004.

87   John Prince-Smith, "On the Significance of Freedom of Trade in World Politics," Address to the Third Congress of German Economists, Köln, 1860, in E. K. Bramsted and K. J. Melhuish, eds., *Western Liberalism: A History in Documents from Locke to Croce,* op. cit., pp. 357–59, p. 357.

88   Montesquieu, *The Spirit of the Laws*, trans. Anne M. Cohler, Basia

Carolyn Miller, and Harold Samuel Stone (1748; Cambridge: Cambridge University Press, 1989), Book 20, "On the laws in their relation to commerce, considered in its nature and its distinctions," Chapter 2, "On the spirit of commerce," p. 338.

89   Carlos W. Polachek and Carlos Seiglie, "Trade, Peace and Democracy: An Analysis of Dyadic Dispute," Institute for the Study of Labor (IZA) Discussion Paper 2170 (June 2006), available at http://papers.ssrn.com/sol3/papers.cfm?abstract_id=915360##.

90   See Erik Gartzke, Quan Li, and Charles Boehmer, "Investing in Peace: Economic Interdependence and International Conflict," *International Organization*, Vol. 55, No. 2 (Spring 2001), pp. 391–438.

91   See Douglas A. Irwin, *Peddling Protectionism: Smoot-Hawley and the Great Depression* (Princeton: Princeton University Press, 2011).

92   Available at http://econjwatch.org/articles/economists-against-smoot-hawley.

93   Harry S. Truman, "Address on Foreign Economic Policy, Delivered at Baylor University, March 6, 1947," Public Papers of the Presidents, Harry S. Truman 1947–53, available at http://trumanlibrary.org/publicpapers/index.php?pid=2193&st=&st1=.

94   Homer, *The Odyssey*, trans. by Robert Fagles (New York: Penguin, 1997), p. 215.

95   Parker T. Moon, *Imperialism and World Politics* (New York: The MacMillan Company, 1926), p. 58. It is well worth reading Moon's description of the cruel exploitation of the Belgian Congo, the so-called "Free State," by King Leopold, which caused unimaginable suffering among the indigenous population, enriched the king, and cost the Belgian taxpayers. The action of the heroic Sir Roger Casement in bringing the horrors of the Congo to the attention of the people of Belgium in the Casement Report of 1904 should be forever remembered. Sadly, after being a hero to the public for exposing such crimes in Congo and Brazil, he was executed by the British government for his active support of Irish independence.

96   See Tom G. Palmer, "Myths of Individualism," *Cato Policy Report* (September/October 1996), available at http://www.libertarianism.org/publications/essays/myths-individualism.

97   Quoted in Johan Hari, "The Two Churchills," review of *Churchill's Empire: The World That Made Him and the World He Made*, by Richard Toye, *New York Times*, 12 August 2010.

98   Josh Sanburn, "Paul Krugman: An Alien Invasion Could Fix the Economy," *Time*, 16 August 2011.

99 Thomas Jefferson to Elbridge Gerry, 13 May 1797, in Julian P. Boyd, et al., eds., *The Papers of Thomas Jefferson*, 36 vols. to date (Princeton, N.J., 1950–), Vol. 29, p. 364.

100 Benjamin Franklin to Jonathan Shipley, 10 June 1782, in Leonard W. Labaree, et al., eds., *The Papers of Benjamin Franklin*, 40 vols. to date (New Haven, Conn.: Yale University Press, 1959–2011), Vol. 37, p. 457.

101 James Madison, *Political Observations*, 20 April 1795, in William T. Hutchinson, et al., eds., *The Papers of James Madison: Congressional Series*, 17 vols. (Charlottesville, Va.: University Press of Virginia, 1962–91), Vol. 15, p. 518.

102 The Declaration of Independence as Adopted by Congress, 4 July 1776, in Boyd, et al., eds., *The Papers of Thomas Jefferson,* Vol. 1, p. 429–30.

103 Bernard Bailyn, *The Ideological Origins of the American Revolution* (Cambridge, Mass.: Harvard University Press, 1967), pp. 36, 48, 61–65, 84, 112–19; Richard H. Kohn, *Eagle and Sword: The Federalists and the Creation of the Military Establishment in America, 1783–1802* (New York: The Free Press), 1–13; Joseph J. Ellis, *His Excellency: George Washington* (New York: Alfred A. Knopf, 2004), pp. 68–72.

104 John Adams to Abigail Adams, 2 September 1777, in L. H. Butterfield, et al., eds., *The Adams Family Correspondence*, 9 vols. to date (Cambridge, Mass.: Harvard University Press, 1963-), Vol. 2, p. 336; Charles Royster, *A Revolutionary People at War: The Continental Army and American Character, 1775–1783* (Chapel Hill, N.C.: University of North Carolina Press, 1979), pp. 116–19, 179–89.

105 George Washington to Lewis Nicola, 22 May 1782, in John C. Fitzpatrick, ed., *The Writings of George Washington*, 39 vols. (Washington, D.C.: U.S. Government Printing Office, 1931–39), Vol. 24, pp. 272–73; Ellis, *His Excellency*, pp. 138–39.

106 Kohn, *Eagle and Sword*, pp. 17–39; Ellis, *His Excellency*, pp. 141–46.

107 Garry Wills, *Cincinnatus: George Washington and the Enlightenment* (Garden City, N.Y.: Doubleday, 1984); George Washington to David Humphreys, 25 July 1785, in W. W. Abbot, et al., eds., *The Papers of George Washington: Confederation Series*, 6 vols. (Charlottesville, Va.: University of Virginia Press, 1992–95), Vol. 3, pp. 148–49.

108 Stuart Leibiger, *Founding Friendship: George Washington, James Madison, and the Creation of the American Republic* (Charlottesville, Va.: University Press of Virginia, 1999), pp. 58–95.

109   Joseph J. Ellis, *Founding Brothers: The Revolutionary Generation* (New York: Alfred A. Knopf, 2001), pp. 120–22, 134–48; George Washington, Farewell Address, 19 September 1796, Founders Online, National Archives (http://founders.archives.gov/documents/ Washington/99-01-02-00963, ver. 2013-12-27).

110   Thomas Jefferson, First Inaugural Address, 4 March 1801, in Julian P. Boyd, et al., eds., *The Papers of Thomas Jefferson*, 36 vols. to date (Princeton, N.J.: Princeton University Press, 1950–), Vol. 33, pp. 150.

111   Ellis, *Founding Brothers*, pp. 190–93; U.S. Const. amend. I. See also James Morton Smith, *Freedom's Fetters: The Alien and Sedition Laws and American Civil Liberties* (Ithaca, N.Y.: Cornell University Press, 1956).

112   David N. Mayer, *The Constitutional Thought of Thomas Jefferson* (Charlottesville, Va.: University Press of Virginia, 1994), pp. 215–18, 244–51; Drew R. McCoy, *The Elusive Republic: Political Economy in Jeffersonian America* (Ithaca, N.Y.: Cornell University Press, 1980), pp. 195–210; Jefferson to Robert R. Livingston, 18 April 1802, in Merrill D. Peterson, ed., *Thomas Jefferson: Writings* (New York: Library of America, 1984), pp. 1105.

113   Ralph Ketcham, *James Madison: A Biography* (New York: Macmillan, 1971), pp. 585–86; Benjamin Wittes and Ritika Singh, "James Madison, Presidential Power, and Civil Liberties in the War of 1812," in Pietro S. Nivola and Peter J. Kastor, eds., *What So Proudly We Hailed: Essays on the Contemporary Meaning of the War of 1812* (Washington, D.C.: Brookings Institution Press, 2012), pp. 97–121.

114   Jefferson to Madison, 27 April 1809, in J. Jefferson Looney, ed., *The Papers of Thomas Jefferson: Retirement Series*, 7 vols. to date (Princeton, N.J.: Princeton University Press, 2004–), Vol. 1, p. 169; Peter S. Onuf, *Jefferson's Empire: The Language of American Nationhood* (Charlottesville, Va.: University of Virginia Press, 2000), pp. 53–79.

115   The term "physiocrat" is derived from Greek and means "the rule of nature." The thinkers of that school believed that society was self-regulating according to knowable principles, rather than being guided by wise princes.

116   McCoy, *The Elusive Republic*, 86–100; Thomas Paine, *Common Sense*, 1776, in Philip S. Foner, ed., *The Complete Writings of Thomas Paine*, 2 vols. (New York: Citadel Press, 1945), 1:20; Jefferson to William Carmichael, 26 December 1786, in Boyd, et al., eds., *The Papers of Thomas Jefferson*, 10:634.

117   Robert Gates, discussion on Meet the Press, January 19, 2014.

Transcript at http://www.nbcnews.com/id/54117257/ns/
meet_the_press-transcripts/t/january-dianne-feinstein-mike-rogers-
alexis-ohanian-john-wisniewski-rudy-giuliani-robert-gates-newt-
gingrich-andrea-mitchell-harold-ford-jr-nia-malika-henderson/#.
UxdBE1OGfKc .

118 Charles Tilly, *Coercion, Capital, and European States, AD 990–1992*
(Cambridge, MA: Blackwell, 1990).

119 For a comprehensive but concise discussion, see Jack S. Levy and
William R. Thompson, *The Arc of War: Origins, Escalation, and
Transformation* (Chicago: University of Chicago Press, 2011).

120 Charles Tilly, "Reflections on the History of European State-Making,"
in Charles Tilly, ed., *The Formation of National States in Western
Europe* (Princeton: Princeton University Press, 1975), p. 42.

121 Jack S. Levy, "Historical Trends in Great Power War, 1495–1975,"
International Studies Quarterly 26, no. 2 (June 1982): 278–300.

122 John Mueller, *Retreat from Doomsday: The Obsolescence of Major
War* (New York: Basic Books, 1989), pp. 240–44.

123 See discussion in Benjamin H. Friedman, Brendan Rittenhouse
Green, and Justin Logan, "Debating American Engagement: The
Future of U.S. Grand Strategy," *International Security* 38, no. 2 (Fall
2013): 183–92.

124 Kenneth N. Waltz, "Waltz Responds to Sagan," in Scott D. Sagan
and Kenneth N. Waltz, *The Spread of Nuclear Weapons: A Debate*
(New York: W. W. Norton, 1995), p. 111.

125 One could suggest that the Israeli strike against the reactor facility
in Syria is a counterargument, but the Syrian program was decades
away from fruition and the Israeli strike accordingly produced
dubious gains for Israeli security.

126 Artemy Kalinovsky, "Decision-Making and the Soviet War in
Afghanistan: From Intervention to Withdrawal," *Journal of Cold
War Studies* 11, no. 4 (Fall 2009): 50.

127 Daryl G. Press, *Calculating Credibility: How Leaders Assess Military
Threats* (Ithaca, NY: Cornell University Press, 2007).

128 See discussion in Alan J. Kuperman, "A Model Humanitarian
Intervention? Reassessing NATO's Libya Campaign," *International
Security* 38, no. 1 (Summer 2013): 105–36.

129 Helene Cooper and Steven Lee Myers, "Obama Takes Hard Line
with Libya After Shift by Clinton," *New York Times*, March 18, 2011.

130 See discussion in Alan J. Kuperman, "A Model Humanitarian
Intervention? Reassessing NATO's Libya Campaign."

131 For an incisive treatment of the Western tendency to ignore politics and the problems this can cause, see Richard K. Betts, "The Delusion of Impartial Intervention," *Foreign Affairs* 73, no. 6 (Nov/Dec 1994): 20–33.

132 President Dwight D. Eisenhower, "Farewell Address to the Nation," January 17, 1961. More generally, see Peter Trubowitz, *Defining the National Interest: Conflict and Change in American Foreign Policy* (Chicago: University of Chicago Press, 1998).

133 Benjamin H. Friedman and Justin Logan, "Why the U.S. Military Budget Is Foolish and Sustainable," *Orbis* 56, issue 2 (Fall 2012): 177–91.

134 On elite politics and overexpansion, see Jack Snyder, *Myths of Empire: Domestic Politics and International Ambition* (Ithaca, NY: Cornell University Press, 1991).

135 In making the case for the Iraq war in the 2003 State of the Union Address, for instance, US President George W. Bush deployed words from a gospel hymn, replacing Christ with the American people. See Alan Cooperman, "Openly Religious, to a Point," *Washington Post*, September 16, 2004. More generally, see Conor Cruise O'Brien, *God Land: Reflections on Religion and Nationalism* (Cambridge, MA: Harvard University Press, 1999).

136 A great deal of the data on SWAT team use was gathered by Professor Peter Kraska. The most systematic data collection went up to 2005. A recent review of the issue can be found in "Paramilitary Police: Cops or Soldiers?" The Economist, March 22, 2014, http://www.economist.com/news/united-states/21599349-americas-police-have-become-too-militarised-cops-or-soldiers.

137 *Presocratic Philosophers: A Critical History with a Selection of Texts*, by G. S. Kirk, J. E. Raven, and M. Schofield (second edition: Cambridge: Cambridge University Press, 1957), p. 193. Heraclitus is also quoted as stating, "Εἰδέναι δὲ χρὴ τὸν πόλεμον ἐόντα ξυνὸν καὶ δίκην ἔριν, καὶ γινόμενα πάντα κατ᾽ ἔριν καὶ χρεών." "It is necessary to know that war is common and right is strife and that all things happen by strife and necessity." (p. 193)

138 Joseph de Maistre, *Considerations on France*, trans. by Richard A. Lebrun (1797; Cambridge: Cambridge University Press, 2000), p. 23.

139 Steven Pinker, *The Better Angels of Our Nature: A History of Violence and Humanity* (London: Penguin Books, 2011). Pinker's book is an excellent example of serious social science, which seeks out and

presents evidence, suggests and tests explanatory hypotheses, and acknowledges uncertainty when dispositive evidence is lacking.

140 Pinker deals with the obvious objection that the twentieth century saw horrifying, staggering, sickening levels of state-organized violence; even taking those into account, the human likelihood of experiencing violence overall declined during the twentieth century. See *The Better Angels of Our Nature: A History of Violence and Humanity*, pp. 233–78.

141 *Ibid.*, p. 769.

142 The terms are used interchangeably in this essay. Libertarianism is known in most countries as "liberalism" or as "classical liberalism" to avoid confusion with how the term liberalism is used in the US. The economist Joseph Schumpeter noted that in the United States, "as a supreme, if unintended, compliment, the enemies of the system of private enterprise have thought it wise to appropriate its label." Joseph Schumpeter, *History of Economic Analysis* (New York: Oxford University Press, 1974), p. 394. See also George H. Smith, *The System of Liberty: Themes in the History of Classical Liberalism* (Cambridge: Cambridge University Press, 2013), esp. chap 1, "Liberalism, Old and New." The history of the word liberalism is described in Guillaume de Bertier de Sauvigny, "Le libéralism. Aux origines d'un mot," *Commentaire*, no. 7 (Autumn), pp. 420–24, p. 420, available online at http://www.commentaire. fr/pdf/articles/1979-3-007/1979-3-007.pdf.

143 John Locke, *Two Treatises of Government*, Peter Laslett, ed. (Cambridge: Cambridge University Press, 1988), II, Chap. VI, § 57, p. 507

144 For a useful overview, see *The English Levellers*, Andrew Sharp, ed. (Cambridge: Cambridge University Press, 1998).

145 "To every individual in nature is given an individual property by nature not to be invaded or usurped by any. For every one, as he is himself, so he has a self-propriety, else could he not be himself; and of this no second may presume to deprive any of without manifest violation of the very principles of nature and of the rules of equity and justice between man and man. Mine and thine cannot be, except this be. No man has power over my rights and liberties, and I over no man's. I may be but an individual, enjoy my self and my self propriety and may right myself no more than myself, or presume any further; if I do, I am an encroacher and an invader upon another man's right—to which I have no right. For by natural birth all men

are equally and alike born to like propriety, liberty, and freedom; and as we are delivered of God by the hand of nature into this world, every one with a natural, innate freedom and propriety—as it were writ in the table of every man's heart, never to be obliterated—even so are we to live, everyone equally and alike to enjoy his birthright and privilege; even all whereof God by nature has made him free." Richard Overton, "An Arrow against All Tyrants and Tyranny," in *The English Levellers*, Andrew Sharp, ed., p. 55.

146 Montesquieu, *The Spirit of the Laws*, Anne M. Cohler, Basia Carolyn Miller, and Harold Samuel Stone, trans. (1748; Cambridge: Cambridge University Press, 1989), Book 20, Chapter 1, p. 338. On property and liberty, see Book 25, Chapter 15, pp. 510–11, among other places.

147 See for a discussion of "catallaxy" as "market order," F. A. Hayek, *Law, Legislation, and Liberty, Vol. 2, The Mirage of Social Justice* (Chicago: University of Chicago Press, 1978) p. 108, citing Liddell and Scott, *A Greek-English Dictionary*.

148 Frédéric Bastiat, "To the Youth of France," in Frédéric Bastiat, *Economic Harmonies*, W. Hayden Boyers, trans. (Irvington-on-Hudson: Foundation for Economic Education, 1964), p. xxiv.

149 Frédéric Bastiat, *ibid.*, p. xxv.

150 Ernst Jünger, *The Storm of Steel, from the Diary of a German Storm-Troop Officer on the Western Front* (New York: Howard Fertig, 1996), pp. 316–17.

151 Joseph de Maistre, *Considerations on France*, op. cit, p. 29.

152 *Ibid.*, p. 31.

153 See Isaiah Berlin, "The Counter-Enlightenment," in Isaiah Berlin, *The Proper Study of Mankind: An Anthology of Essays* (New York: Farrar, Straus and Giroux, 1998), pp. 243–68.

154 Steven Pinker, *The Better Angels of Our Nature*, p. 226.

155 Friedrich Engels, "Outlines of a Critique of Political Economy," in Lawrence S. Stepelevich, ed., *The Young Hegelians: An Anthology* (Amherst, N.Y.: Humanity Books, 1999), pp. 278–302, p. 283.

156 John Ruskin, "War," Lecture delivered at the Royal Military Academy, Woolwich, in *The Crown of Wild Olive, Munera Pulveris, Sesame and Lilies*, by John Ruskin (New York: Thomas Y. Crowell & Co., n.d.), pp. 66–67. Ruskin added that "The common notion that peace and the virtues of civil life flourished together, I found, to be wholly untenable. Peace and the *vices* of civil life only flourish together. We talk of peace and learning, and of peace and plenty, and

of peace and civilisation; but I found that those were not the words which the Muse of History coupled together: that on her lips, the words were—peace and sensuality, peace and selfishness, peace and corruption, peace and death. I found, in brief, that all great nations learned their truth of word, and strength of thought, in war; that they were nourished in war, and wasted by peace; taught by war, and deceived by peace; trained by war, and betrayed by peace;—in a word, that they were born in war, and expired in peace." (p. 70)

157 In his *Letters Concerning the English Nation*, Voltaire described his experience of more liberal and commercial England (in comparison to France) and observed that

> tho' the Episcopal and Presbyterian sects are the two prevailing ones in *Great-Britain*, yet all others are very welcome to come and settle in it, and live very sociably together, tho' most of their preachers hate one another almost as cordially as a Jansenist damns a Jesuit.
>
> Take a view of the *Royal-Exchange* in *London*, a place more venerable than many courts of justice, where the representatives of all nations meet for the benefit of mankind. There the Jew, the Mahometan, and the Christian transact together as tho' they all profess'd the same religion, and give the name of Infidel to none but bankrupts. There the Presbyterian confides in the Anabaptist, and the Churchman depends on the Quaker's word. At the breaking up of this pacific and free assembly, some withdraw to the synagogue, and others to take a glass. This man goes and is baptiz'd in a great tub, in the name of the Father, Son, and Holy Ghost: That man has his son's foreskin cut off, whilst a sett of *Hebrew* words (quite unintelligible to him) are mumbled over his child. Others retire to their churches, and there wait for the inspiration of heaven with their hats on, and all are satisfied.

Voltaire, *Letters Concerning the English Nation* (1733; Oxford: Oxford University Press, 1994), Letter VI, "On the Presbyterians," p. 30.

158 Karl Marx and Friedrich Engels, *The Communist Manifesto* (1848; London: Verso, 2012), p. 37.

159 Robert Musil, *The Man Without Qualities*, Vol. I, trans. by Sophie Wilkins (New York: Vintage Books, 1995), p. 22.

160 Karl Marx and Frederick Engels, *ibid.*, pp. 34–35.

161 As Marx put it, "by 'individual' you mean no other person than the bourgeois, than the middle-class owner of property. This person must, indeed, be swept out of the way, and made impossible." (*Communist Manifesto*, p. 55) For a critique of the Marxian theory of class conflict, see "Classical Liberalism, Marxism, and the Conflict of Classes: The Classical Liberal Theory of Class Conflict," in Tom G. Palmer, *Realizing Freedom: Libertarian Theory, History, and Practice* (second edition: Washington, D.C.: Cato Institute, 2014). The realization of the vision of class conflict through the elimination of class enemies, combined with the disastrous efforts to eliminate property rights, market exchange, and the price system, was responsible for many tens of millions of deaths in the twentieth century. The theory, of course, was that a new and universal class, the proletariat, would take over and class conflict would disappear, but the reality was that a new class system was created and both internal and external conflicts were perpetuated by the need to identify and combat ever more enemies, all of whom were designated bourgeois or agents of the bourgeoisie.

162 As Italian Fascist theorist Giovanni Gentile put it, Fascism originated as a doctrine of the unity of the nation through war: "entry into the war [World War I] was necessary in order to finally unite the nation through the shedding of blood. . . . The war was seen as a way to cement the nation as only war can, creating a single thought for all citizens, a single feeling, a single passion, and a common hope, an anxiety lived by all, day by day—with the hope that the life of the individual might be seen and felt as connected, obscurely or vividly, with the life that is common to all—but which transcends the particular interests of any. The war was sought in order to bring the nation together—in order to render it a true nation, real, alive, capable of acting, and ready to make itself valued and of consequence in the world—to enter into history with its own personality, with its own form, with its own character, with its own originality, never again to live on the borrowed culture of others and in the shadow of those great people who make history. To create, therefore, a true nation, in the only way the creation of every spiritual reality is undertaken: with effort and through sacrifice." Giovanni Gentile, *Origins and Doctrine of Fascism*, trans. by A. James Gregor (New Brunswick, NJ: Transaction Publishers, 2007), p. 2.

163 Adolf Hitler *Mein Kampf* ("My Struggle") Ralph Mannheim, trans. (Boston: Houghton Mifflin, 1943), p. 289.

164 David Held, *Introduction to Critical Theory: Horkheimer to Habermas* (Berkeley: University of California Press, 1980), p. 160 [citing Nietzsche].

165 Herbert Marcuse, "Repressive Tolerance," in Robert P. Wolff, Barrington Moore, Jr., and Herbert Marcuse, *A Critique of Pure Tolerance* (Boston: Beacon Press, 1965).

166 There has been a proliferation of academic subspecialties claiming to promote various struggles against cultural hegemony, commodification, objectification, and so on. There may be worth in the study of such topics, for much of human history has been characterized by conflict and domination. The question is whether conflict can be reduced, ameliorated, or resolved, or is innate to humanity or perhaps even constitutive of human beings as such. An example of one school that rejects liberalism, equal rights, freedom of speech, and toleration is the movement that has been termed "gender feminism" (mainly by its critics), a leading theorist of which is Catherine MacKinnon, who promotes criminalization of pornography and prosecution and jailing of those who produce, market, or purchase it. According to MacKinnon, "Sexuality . . . is a form of power. Gender, as socially constructed, embodies it, not the reverse. Women and men are divided by gender, made into the sexes as we know them, by the social requirements of heterosexuality, which institutionalizes male sexual dominance and female sexual submission." Catherine A. MacKinnon, "Feminism, Marxism, Method, and the State: An Agenda for Theory," *Signs*, Vol. 7, No. 3, Feminist Theory (Spring 1982), pp. 515–44, p. 533. In *Toward a Feminist Theory of the State* (Cambridge, Ma.: Harvard University Press, 1989), she rejects "gender neutrality" and "individual rights" on the grounds that "Abstract equality *necessarily* [emphasis added] reinforces the inequalities of the status quo to the extent that it evenly reflects an unequal social arrangement" (p. 227) and "Taking the sexes 'as individuals,' meaning one at a time, as if they do not belong to genders, perfectly obscures these collective realities and substantive correlates of gender group status behind the mask of recognition of individual rights." (p. 228) See also her equalization of all male-female relationships to the status of rape in her essay "Crimes of War, Crimes of Peace," in Stephen Shute and Susan Hurley, eds., *On Human Rights: The Oxford Amnesty Lectures 1993* (New York: Basic Books, 1993), "The fact of Serbian aggression is beyond question, just as the fact of male aggression against women is beyond question, here and everywhere." (p. 87)

167 As Rear-Admiral S. B. Luce wrote in 1891, "War is one of the great

agencies by which human progress is effected. Scourge though it be, and much as its practice is to be deplored, we must still recognize war as the operation of the economic laws of nature for the government of the human family. It stimulates national growth, solves otherwise insoluble problems of domestic and political economy, and purges a nation of its humors." Rear-Admiral S. B. Luce, United States Navy, "The Benefits of War," *The North American Review*, Vol. 153, No. 421, Dec. 1891.

168 William Kristol and Robert Kagan, "Toward a Neo-Reaganite Foreign Policy," *Foreign Affairs*, July/August 1996, available at http://www.foreignaffairs.com/articles/52239/william-kristol-and-robert-kagan/toward-a-neo-reaganite-foreign-policy.

169 Samuel Huntington posited a "clash of civilizations" in *The Clash of Civilizations and the Remaking of World Order* (New York: Simon & Schuster, 1997), p. 207: "Civilizations are the ultimate human tribes, and the clash of civilizations is tribal conflict on a global scale. In the emerging world, states and groups from two different civilizations may form limited, ad hoc, tactical connections and coalitions to advance their interests against entities from a third civilization or for other shared purposes. Relations between groups from different civilizations however will be almost never close, usually cool, and often hostile." (p 207)

170 See, for example, G. A. Cohen, "Freedom, Justice and Capitalism," *New Left Review*, I/126 (March–April 1981), pp. 3–16.

171 Sir Robert Filmer, "Observations upon Aristotle's Politiques," in Filmer, *Patriarcha and Other Writings*, ed. by Johann P. Sommerville (Cambridge: Cambridge University Press, 1991), p. 275. John Locke, an early figure in the articulation of modern libertarian ideas, responded that, "[F]reedom is not, as we are told [by Filmer], *A liberty for every Man to do what he lists:* (For who could be free, when every other Man's Humour might domineer over him?) But a *Liberty* to dispose, and order, as he lists, his Persons, Actions, Possessions, and his whole Property, within the Allowance of those Laws under which he is; and therein not to be subject to the arbitrary Will of another, but freely follow his own." John Locke, *Two Treatises of Government*, ed. Peter Laslett [Cambridge: Cambridge University Press, 1988], II, chap VI, §57, p. 306.

172 The speciousness of the claim is evident when one considers the perspective of the rape victim, not merely in physical terms, but in terms of the victim's desires regarding the one body the victim has

and whether the victim is to make choices regarding that body, or it is to be subject to the desires of any and all who may desire it. Moreover, a decline in rape is not, from the perspective of freedom, completely equivalent to an increase in rape, on the grounds that one restraint (preventing rape) balances out the other (perpetrating rape).

173 Jan-Werner Müller, *A Dangerous Mind: Carl Schmitt in Post-War European Thought* (New Haven: Yale University Press, 2003), p. 1. Franz Oppenheimer and Joseph Schumpeter, two prominent classical liberals who wrote in German, were singled out for strenuous attack in *The Concept of the Political* (pp. 76–79).

174 Carl Schmitt, *The Concept of the Political*, Georg Schwab, trans. and ed. (1932; Chicago: University of Chicago Press, 2007), p. 26.

175 See Aleksandr Dugin, *The Fourth Political Theory* (London: Arktos, 2012), which incorporates the major elements of National Socialist theory, with the exception of the anti-Semitism (homosexuals and Americans provide the substitute), including heavy reliance on Schmitt's theories of "Great Spaces."

176 Carl Schmitt, *The Concept of the Political*, p. 28.

177 Carl Schmitt, *The Concept of the Political*, p. 35. "The state as the decisive political entity possesses an enormous power: the possibility of waging war and thereby publicly disposing of the lives of men. The *jus belli* contains such a disposition. It implies a double possibility: the right to demand from its own members the readiness to die and unhesitatingly to kill enemies." (p. 46)

178 Slavoj Žižek, "Carl Schmitt in the Age of Post-Politics," in *The Challenges of Carl Schmitt*, Chantal Mouff ed. (London: Verso, 1999), pp. 18–37, p. 29.

179 John Rawls, *Political Liberalism* (New York: Columbia University Press, 1993), p. 267.

180 Saul Anton, "Enemies: A Love Story," *Lingua Franca*, May/June, 2000.

181 See the treatment in Jan-Werner Müller, *A Dangerous Mind: Carl Schmitt in Post-War European Thought,* pp. 229–32.

182 Michael Hardt and Antonio Negri, *Empire* (Cambridge, Ma.: Harvard University Press, 2001), p. 45–46. The prefiguration of the attack by Osama bin-Laden's suicide bombers on the Twin Towers and the Pentagon may have been one reason the book sank below the waves shortly after the attacks. See Lorraine Adams, "A Global Theory Spins on an Altered Axis: 'Empire' Author Michael Hardt in

Wake of Attacks," *Washington Post*, September 29, 2001. In their book, Hardt and Negri speculate that "Perhaps the more capital extends its global networks of production and control, the more powerful any singular point of revolt can be. Simply by focusing their own powers, concentrating their energies in a tense and compact coil, these serpentine struggles strike directly at the highest articulations of imperial order." (p. 58) Hardt and Negri bemoan the growth of international trade and transnational non-state institutions, which they perceive as causing the "decline of any autonomous political sphere." That autonomous political sphere they identify with the nation-state, which does not mean for them a rejection of Schmitt's thesis, but a confirmation, for the confrontation of friend with enemy for them persists, but merely moved to "a supranational level." (pp. 307–9) Moreover, in typically convoluted language, they call for absolute and complete suppression of freedom of speech: "The real revolutionary practice refers to the level of *production*. Truth will not make us free, but taking control of the production of truth will. Mobility and hybridity are not liberatory, but taking control of the production of mobility and stasis, purities and mixtures is. The real truth commissions of Empire will be constituent assemblies of the multitude, social factories for the production of truth." (p. 156) The erratic and impulsive Marxist writer Slavoj Žižek has embraced Schmitt's approach to argue that even liberal democracy must embrace the "Schmittean" approach, that "our pluralistic and tolerant liberal democracies remain deeply Schmittean: they continue to rely on political *Einbildungskraft* [the transcendental power of imagination] to provide them with the appropriate figure to render visible the invisible Enemy. Far from suspending the binary logic Friend/Enemy, the fact that the Enemy is defined as the fundamentalist opponent of pluralistic tolerance merely adds a reflexive twist to it." Slavoj Žižek, "Are we in a war? Do we have an enemy?," *London Review of Books*, Vol. 24, No. 10, May 23, 2002.

183   Michael Hardt and Antonio Negri, *Empire*, pp. 65–66.

184   George Orwell, "Politics and the English Language," in George Orwell, *A Collection of Essays* (New York: Harcourt, 1981), (p. 167)

185   Carl Schmitt, "The Großraum Order of International Law with a Ban on Intervention for Spatially Foreign Powers: A Contribution to the Concept of Reich in International Law (1939–41)," in Carl Schmitt, *Writings on War*, Timothy Nunan, trans. (London: Polity Press, 2011), pp. 75–124, p. 109.

186   The relationship between Schmitt and Strauss has been discussed in a number of books, many of which dance around the question of Strauss's admiration for fascism. See Leo Strauss, "Notes on Carl Schmitt, The Concept of the Political," postscript to Carl Schmitt, *The Concept of the Political*, pp. 97–122; Heinrich Meier, *Carl Schmitt and Leo Strauss: The Hidden Dialogue* (Chicago: University of Chicago Press, 2006); and C. Bradley Thompson, with Yaron Brook, *Neoconservatism: An Obituary for an Idea* (Boulder: Paradigm Publishers, 2010), esp. chapter 9, "Flirting with Fascism." There is also the matter of Strauss's letter of May 19, 1933 to Karl Löwith, written from Paris after the victory of the National Socialists in Germany. Strauss writes that it is horrible that "the entire German-Jewish intellectual proletariat is here" (in Paris) and that he would most prefer to return to Germany, but, he notes, Jews are no longer welcome in Germany. He added, though, that nothing against the principles of the right follows from the fact that Germany, having turned to the far right, would not tolerate them (Löwith was also Jewish): "daraus, dass das rechts-gewordene Deutschland uns nicht toleriert, folgt schlechterdings nichts gegen die rechten Prinzipien." "To the contrary," he wrote, "only with the principles of the right—fascist, authoritarian, imperial principles—can one fight against the whole miserable mess with decency ('mit Anstand') and without absurd and pathetic appeals to 'the imprescriptible rights of man.'" He added, and this is truly twisting the knife in the corpse of liberalism, that "There is no reason to contritely crawl back on one's knees to the cross [a rich phrase in German that is not so easy to translate, especially as it refers to "the cross" and Strauss was a Jew, which is probably why he used it], and not even to the cross of liberalism, as long as the spark of true Roman ideas still glimmers somewhere in the world; and anyway, better the ghetto than any form of the cross." Letter of May 19, 1933 from Leo Strauss to Karl Löwith, in Leo Strauss, *Gesammelte Schriften, Band 3, Hobbes's politische Wissenschaft und zugehörige Schriften—Briefe*, second revised edition, ed. by Heinrich and Wiebke Meier (Stuttgart: Verlag J. B. Metzler), pp. 624–26. Strauss's defenders, when they have acknowledged the letter, have gone to some pains to explain away what he meant, but it seems far more than likely, given his explicit positive invocation of "fascist, authoritarian, imperial principles" that he was referring to the Fascist state Mussolini had established in Rome. Mussolini was attempting to establish a "New Roman Empire" and was at the

time a rival, not an ally, of Hitler and the National Socialists, and did not (again, at that time) incorporate anti-Semitism into the state ideology.

187 Robert Kagan and William Kristol, "What to Do About Iraq," *The Weekly Standard*, January 21, 2002, available at http://www.weeklystandard.com/Content/Public/Articles/000/000/000/768pylwj.asp

188 David Brooks, "A Return to National Greatness: A Manifesto for a Lost Creed," *The Weekly Standard*, March 3, 1997.

189 William Kristol and Robert Kagan, "Toward a Neo-Reaganite Foreign Policy."

190 Leo Strauss, "Notes on *The Concept of the Political*," reprinted in Carl Schmitt, *The Concept of the Political*, pp. 97–122, p. 122. The influence of Strauss on Schmitt has been described in Heinrich Meier, *Carl Schmitt and Leo Strauss: The Hidden Dialogue*. Those who have brushed off Schmitt's services to the Third Reich as mere careerism or opportunism should read more of Schmitt's suppressed writings, such as "Der Führer Schützt das Recht" ("The Leader Guards/Protects the Law"), published in the *Deutsche Juristen-Zeitung* (August 1, 1934; available at http://www.flechsig.biz/DJZ34_CS.pdf), which was published after Hitler's execution of hundreds of opponents, and the eye-opening (and stomach churning) chapters on Schmitt in Yvonne Sherratt, *Hitler's Philosophers* (New Haven: Yale University Press, 2013) and Emmanuel Faye, *Heidegger: The Introduction of Nazism into Philosophy*, (New Haven: Yale University Press, 2009), as well as Raphael Gross's revelations and analysis in *Carl Schmitt and the Jews: The "Jewish Question," the Holocaust, and German Legal Theory* (Madison: University of Wisconsin Press, 2007).

191 See the discussion in Emmanuel Faye, *Heidegger: The Introduction of Nazism into Philosophy*, *op. cit.*, pp. 158–62.

192 Ludwig von Mises, *Omnipotent Government: The Rise of the Total State and Total War* (1944; Indianapolis: Liberty Fund, 2011), p. 106, available at http://files.libertyfund.org/files/2399/Mises_OmnipotentGovt1579_LFeBk.pdf.

193 Carl Schmitt, *The Concept of the Political*, p. 54.

194 *Ibid.*, p. 55.

195 *Ibid.*, p. 71.

196 *Ibid.*, p. 29.

197 Ernst Jünger, *The Storm of Steel, from the Diary of a German Storm-Troop Officer on the Western Front*, p. 319.

198 The phrase was popularized by the Marxist writer Johann Plenge

in his 1916 book *1789 und 1914: Die symbolischen Jahre in der Geschichte des politischen Geistes*, in which he proclaimed that "under the necessity of war socialist ideas have been driven into German economic life, its organization has grown together into a new spirit, and so the assertion of our nation for mankind has given birth to the idea of 1914, the idea of German organization, the national unit of state socialism." Quoted in F. A. Hayek, *The Road to Serfdom* (1944; London: Routledge & Kegan Paul, 1979), p. 127.

199 *Briefwechsel, Briefe 1930–1983 Ernst Jünger / Carl Schmitt*, Helmut Kiesel, ed. (Stuttgart: Klett-Kotta, 2012)

200 Jünger's 100th birthday was celebrated with a letter from French Socialist president François Mitterand, who had himself switched during the war years from service to the Vichy-Fascist regime to the socialists when it became clear which side was going to win the war. The letter can be found at http://www.ernst-juenger.org/2012/05/francois-mitterand-to-ernst-junger-on.html.

201 Ernst Jünger, *ibid.*, p. 317.

202 Recounted as "We have sentenced you to death because we cannot apprehend your brother. You must suffer for your brother." In Hilton Tims, *Erich Maria Remarque: The Last Romantic* (New York: Carroll & Graf, 2003), p. 143.

203 "Die echte Revolution hat noch gar nicht stattgefunden, sie marschiert unaufhaltsam heran. Sie ist keine Reaktion, sondern eine wirkliche Revolution mit all ihren Kennzeichen und Äußerungen, ihre Idee ist die völkische, zu bisher nicht gekannter Schärfe geschliffen, ihr Banner das Hakenkreuz, ihre Ausdrucksform die Konzentration des Willens in einem einzigen Punkt—die Diktatur! Sie wird ersetzen das Wort durch die Tat, die Tinte durch das Blut, die Phrase durch das Opfer, die Feder durch das Schwert." Ernst Jünger, "Revolution und Idee," *Völkischer Beobachter* (advertised as the "Fighting Paper of the National Socialist Movement of Greater Germany"), September 23/24, 1923, in Helmuth Kiesel, *Ernst Jünger: Die Biographie* (München: Siedler Verlag, 2007), p. 268.

204 Ernst Jünger, "Total Mobilization," trans. Joel Golb & Richard Wolin in Richard Wolin (ed.), *The Heidegger Controversy: A Critical Reader* (Cambridge, MA: MIT Press, 1998), pp. 119–39, p. 127, p. 134. Benito Mussolini had earlier expressed the idea of regimentation as the alternative to liberalism: "The truth, manifest henceforth to all whose eyes are not blinded by dogmatism, is that men are perhaps tired of liberty. They have had an orgy of it. Liberty to-day is no longer the chaste and severe virgin for whom fought and died the

generations of the first half of the past century. For the youths of to-day, intrepid, eager, stern, who envisage the dawn of the new era, there are other words which exercise a more potent fascination and these words are: Order, Hierarchy, Discipline. . . . Be it known then, once and for all, that Fascism knows no idols, worships no fetishes. It has already stepped, and, if need be, will quietly turn around to step once more, over the more or less putrid body of the Goddess Liberty." *The Life of Benito Mussolini*, by Margherita G. Sarfatti, Introduction by Signor Mussolini, Frederic Whyte, trans. (New York: Frederick A. Stokes Company, 1925), pp. 328–29 (quoting an article of May 1923 by Mussolini in the publication *Gerarchia*).

205 In Julien Hervier, *The Details of Time: Conversation with Jünger* (New York: Marsilio Publishers, 1995), p. 69.

206 Vasily Grossman, *Life and Fate: A Novel*, trans by Robert Chandler (New York: Harper & Row, 1987), p. 230.

207 Ernst Jünger, *On Pain*, David C. Durst, trans. (1934; New York: Telos Press Publishing, 2008), p. 17.

208 William Kristol and Robert Kagan, *op. cit*.

209 Charles T. Sprading, *Liberty and the Great Libertarians* (1913; New York: Fox & Wilkes, 1995), p. 29.

210 *Ibid.*, p. 28.

211 E. L. Godkin, "The Eclipse of Liberalism," *The Nation*, August 9, 1900.

Note: An index for the volume is available at http://studentsforliberty.org/peace-love-liberty-index

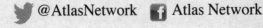

STUDENTS FOR LIBERTY

SFL

Students from 1,369 groups around the world are coming together to fight for their social, economic, and academic freedom. Take back your future by joining the student movement for liberty today!

WWW.STUDENTSFORLIBERTY.ORG

"It is time to celebrate the virtues of peace, of cooperation and industry, of trade and commerce, of science and knowledge, of love and beauty, of liberty and justice, and to leave behind the vices of war, of conflict and destruction, of looting and confiscating, of censoring and stifling, of hatred and horror, of coercion and lawlessness. In the modern world, the world of peace and rising prosperity, the prize should to go to those who call upon human beings to follow peace, rather than war and slaughter."

—Tom Palmer, Editor

Please consider giving copies of *Peace, Love, & Liberty* to students and teachers, local political leaders, business and labor associations, the news media, and to your activist friends all across America. Knowledge is power in political debate. This book will give you that power.

Special Bulk Copy Discount Schedule

1 book	$ 9.95	25 books	$ 75.00	500 books	$ 975.00
5 books	$25.00	50 books	$125.00	1000 books	$1,750.00
10 books	$35.00	100 books	$225.00		

All prices include postage and handling.

JAMESON BOOKS, INC
Post Office Box 738
Ottawa, IL 61350

ORDER TOLL FREE
800-426-1357

Please send me _____ copies of *Peace, Love, & Liberty.*

Enclosed is my check for $ _____
                              or please charge my [ ] MasterCard   [ ] Visa   [ ] Discover

No._____ Ver. Code_____ Exp. Date_____

Signature_____ Telephone _____

Name_____

Address_____

City_____ State_____ Zip_____
Illinois residents please add 6.5% sales tax. Please allow 2 weeks for delivery.